COLORING BOOK

Geometrics and Abstracts

Hours and Hours Of Fun

For Adults and Children

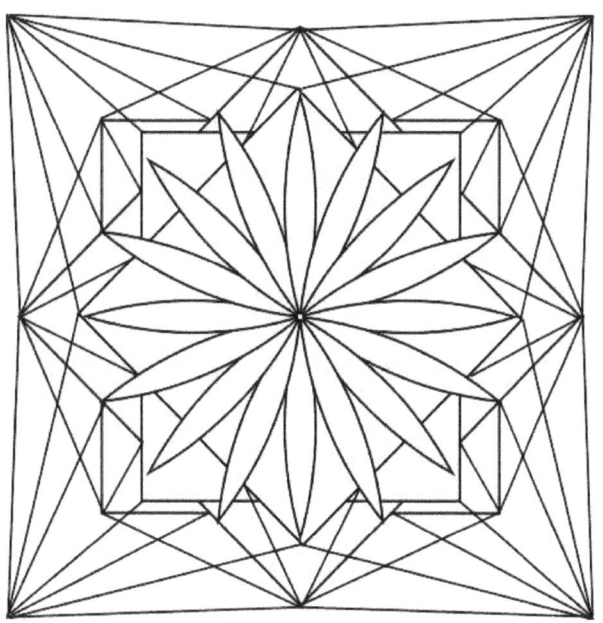

By: Kaye Dennan of

KD Coloring Studio

ISBN-13 978-1517774325

PUBLISHERS NOTES

Disclaimer

Paperback Edition

Manufactured in the United States of America

A note from the Illustrator

Geometrics and Abstracts is a book working with shapes and line widths to create varied and interesting images to color. Working with varied shapes and styles expands ones way of thinking about color and encourages the use of color to create a secondary design within a design.

Discovering your inner artistic pleasure is one of life's happiest moments. It is a creative experience you can enjoy all on your own but one that you can share with others as well.

When you start coloring it is easy to color between the lines and find enjoyment just in the practice of adding color to paper.

As you continue in your discovery you will find that colors talk to each other, they mix and blend and create new emotions.

Colors speak to us too.

Become aware of the affect of colors on your emotions. Take the time to site and understand the change of emotions as you take in colors that you see. When outside look at different colors and recognize your emotion. Look at blocks of color and see if it makes any difference to the way you feel.

Most of us have favorite colors and they are favorites because we like how they make us feel when we see them or even wear them.

Some people even find that their observance of a color a person is wearing affects the way that they initially react to a person: positively, negatively or cautiously.

Geometrics and Abstracts

Basic relationships are listed below but the reality is that what might make one person feel cheerful can make another person feel irritated depending on the viewers' past experiences or cultural differences.

Warm Colors – Red, Orange, Yellow

Cool Colors – Green, Blue, Purple

Neutral Colors – Black, Gray, White, Tan, Brown

I encourage you to experiment with color and shapes and enjoy your coloring pass-time.

****

Every Second Page has been printed with a repeated design so that you do not ruin one of your colored designs with bleeding.

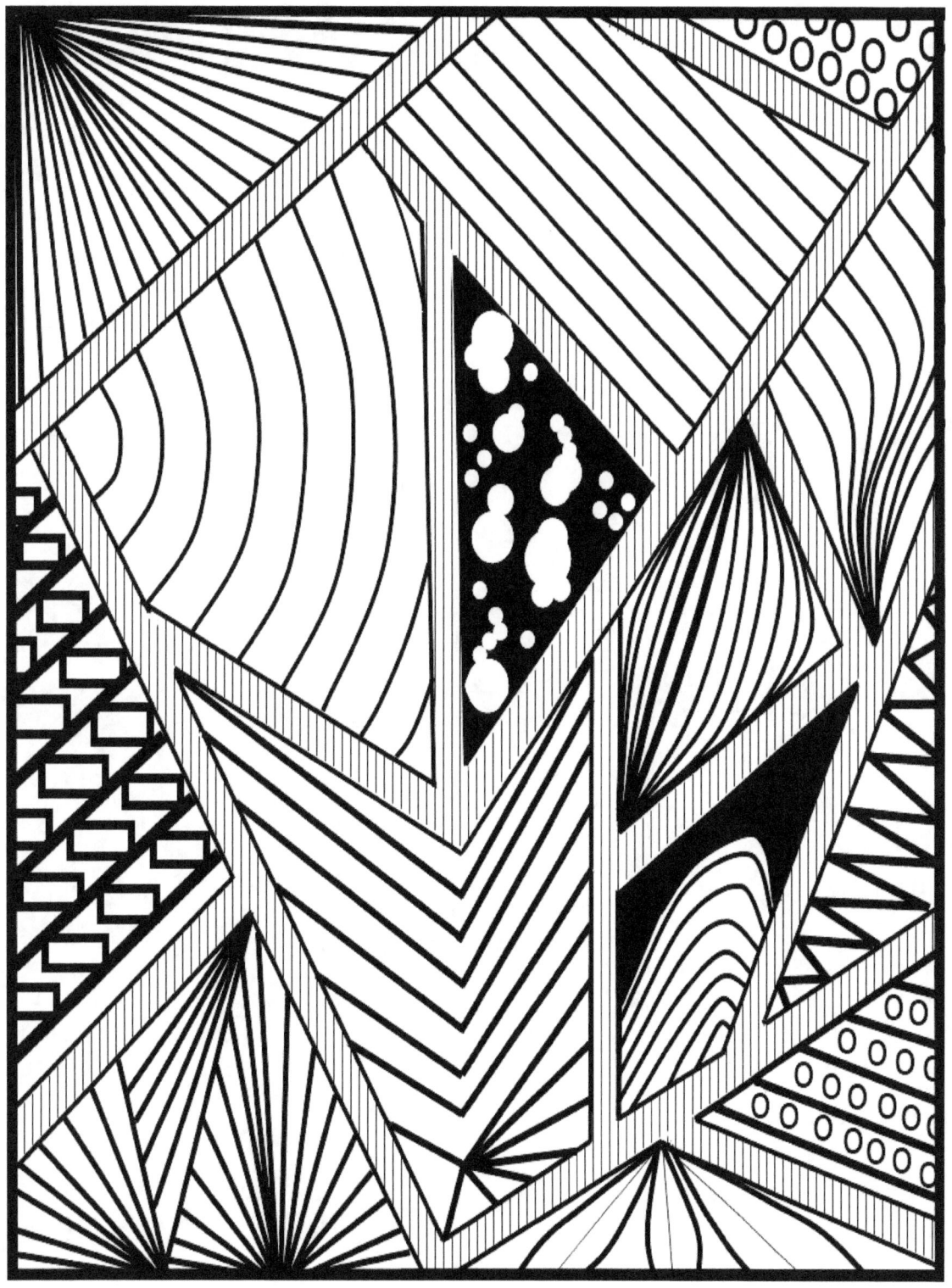

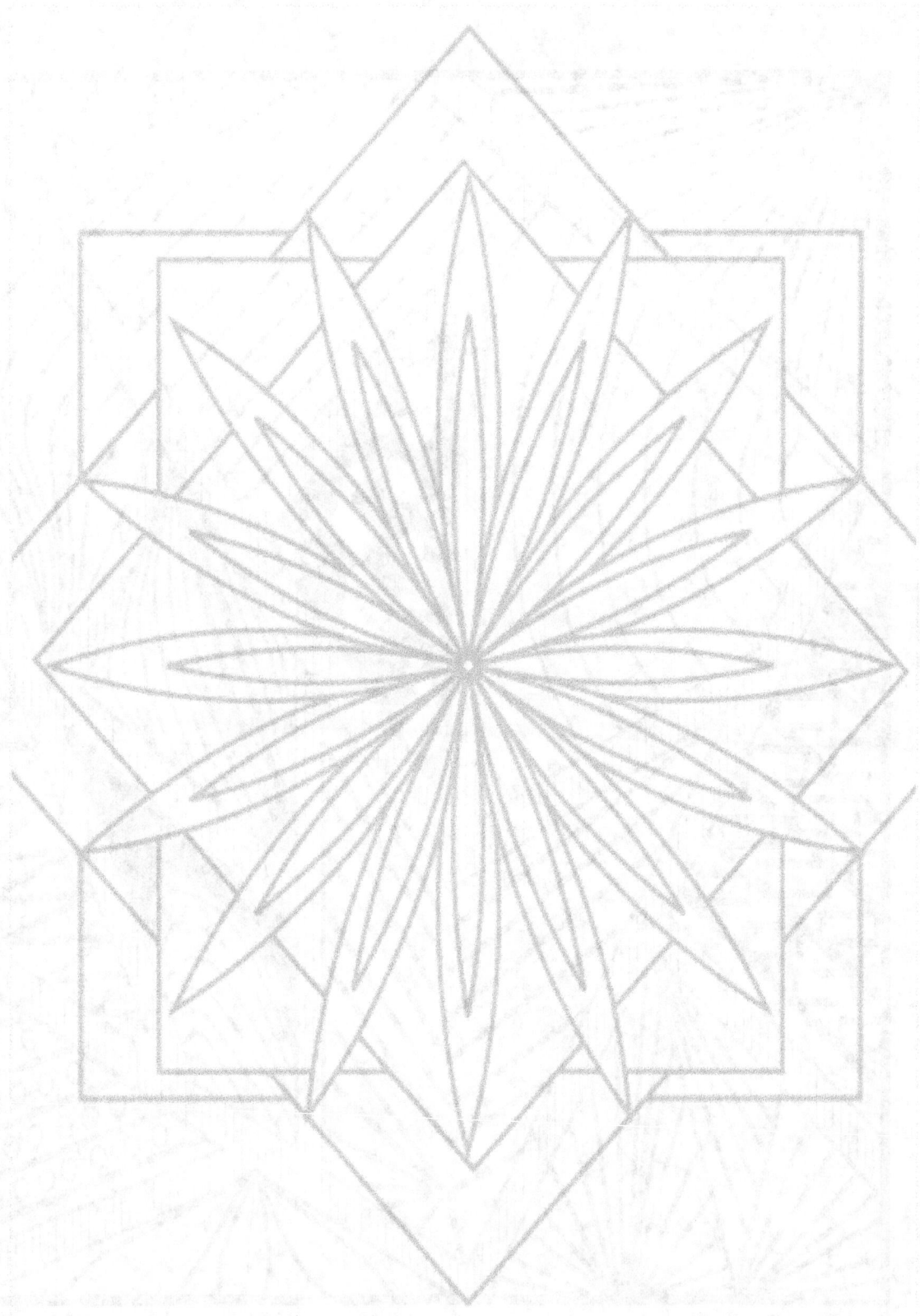

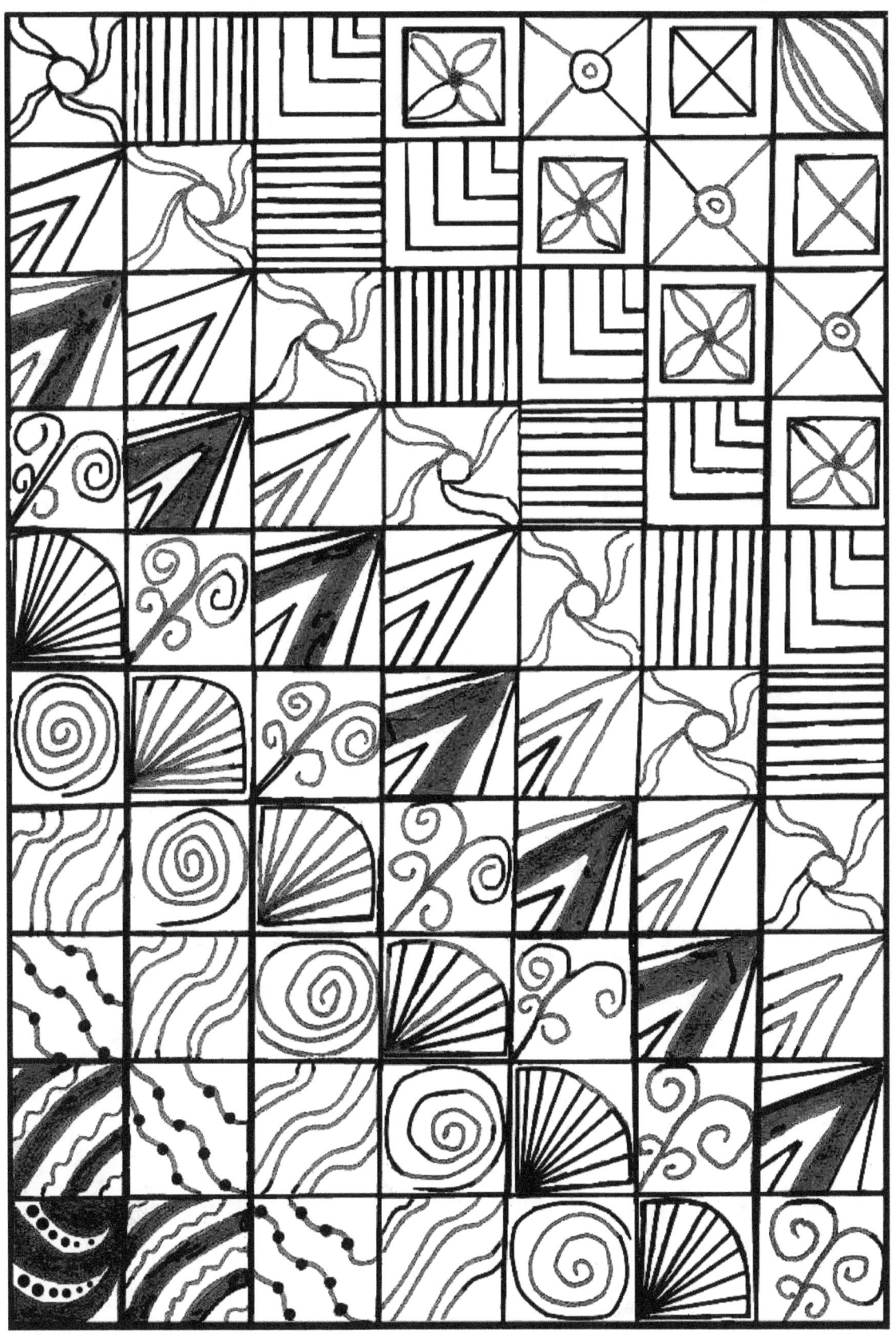

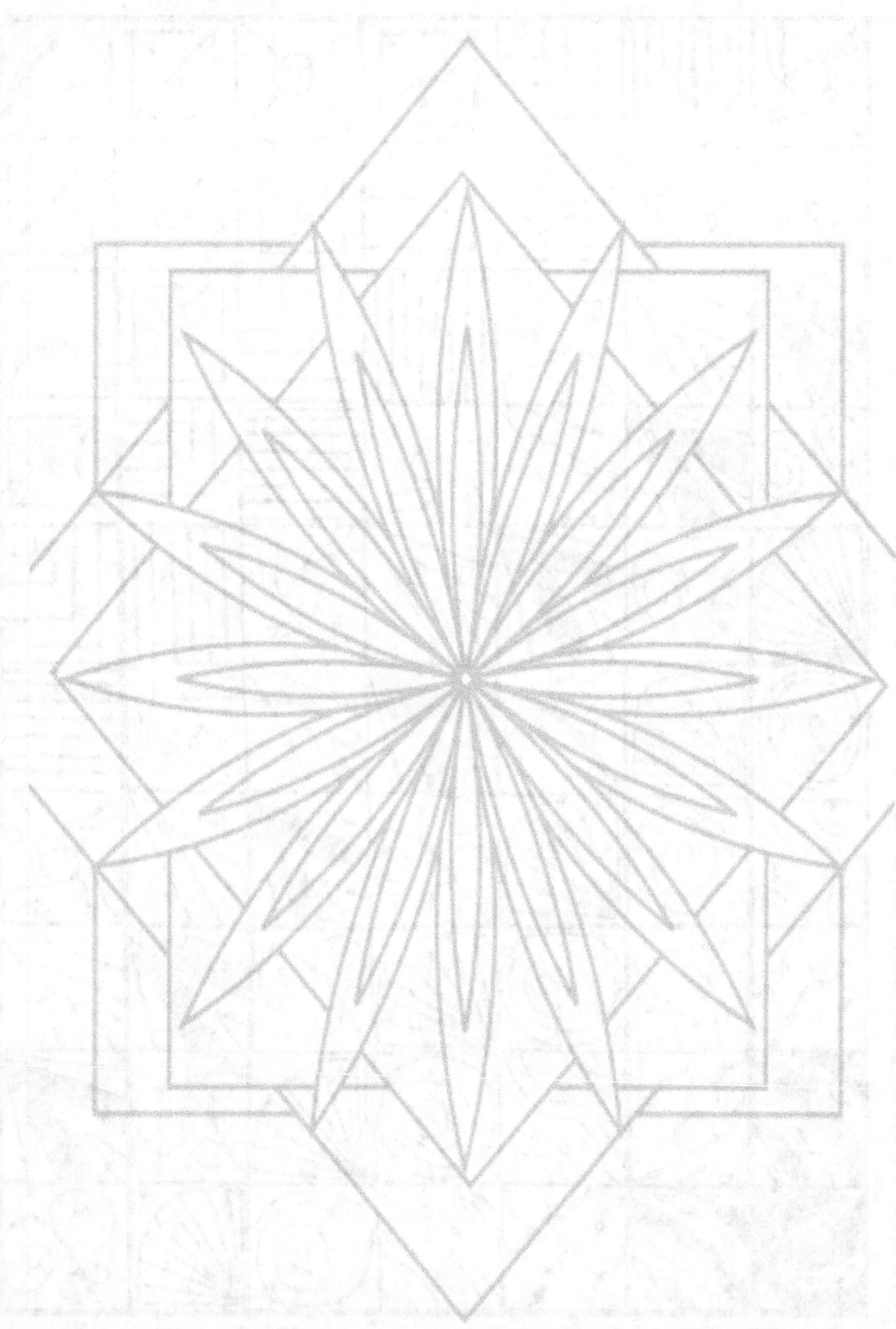

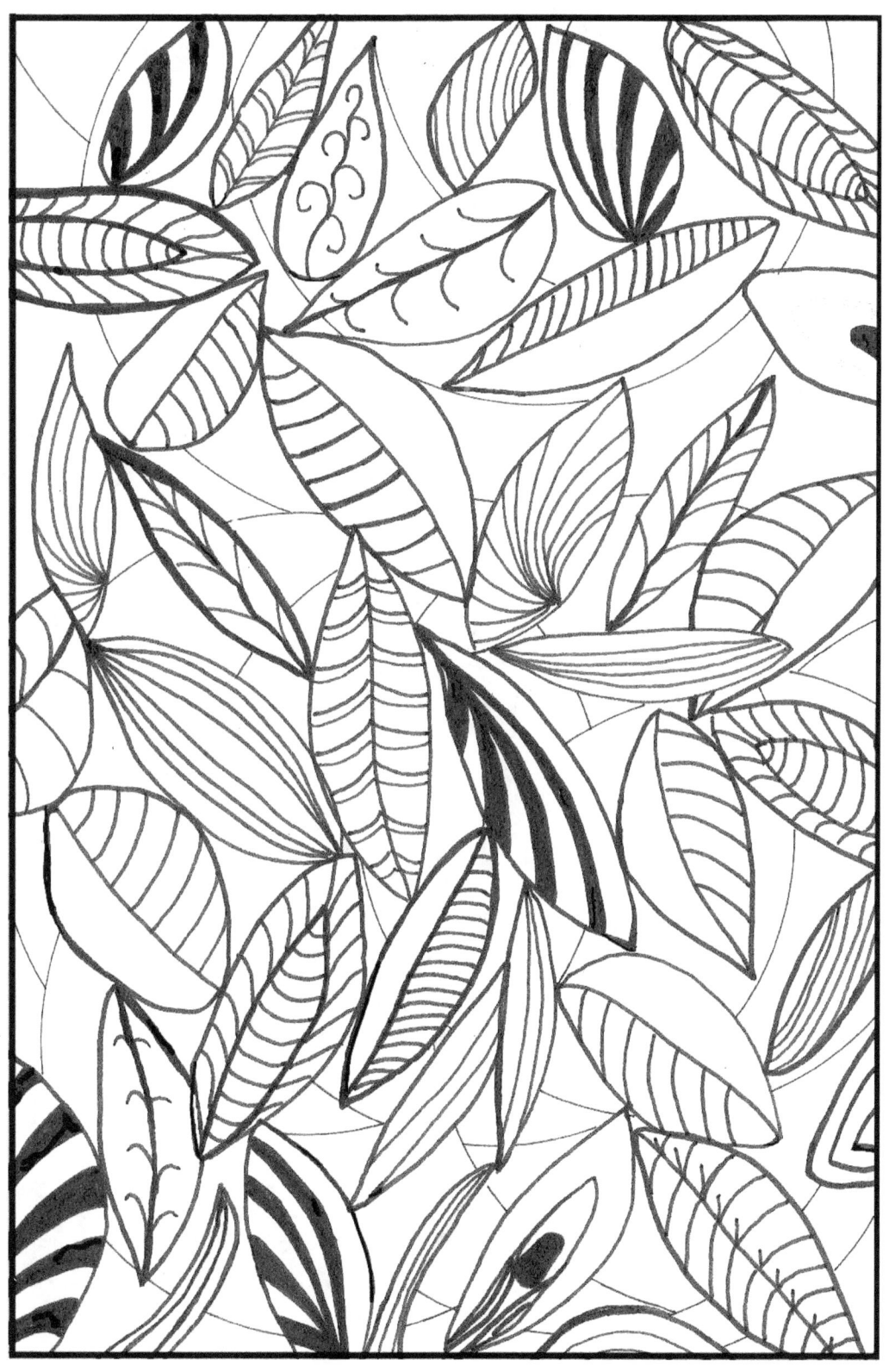

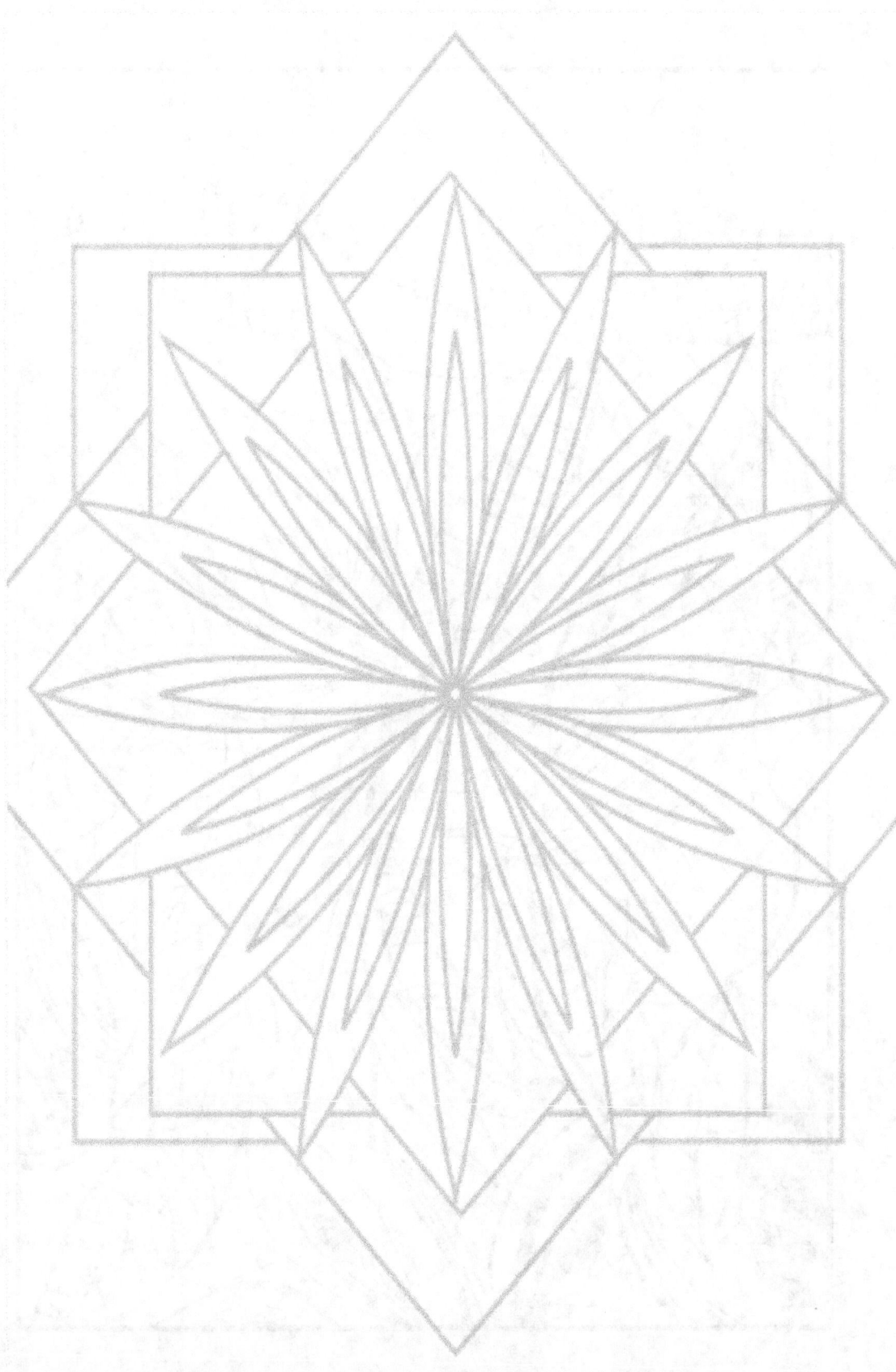

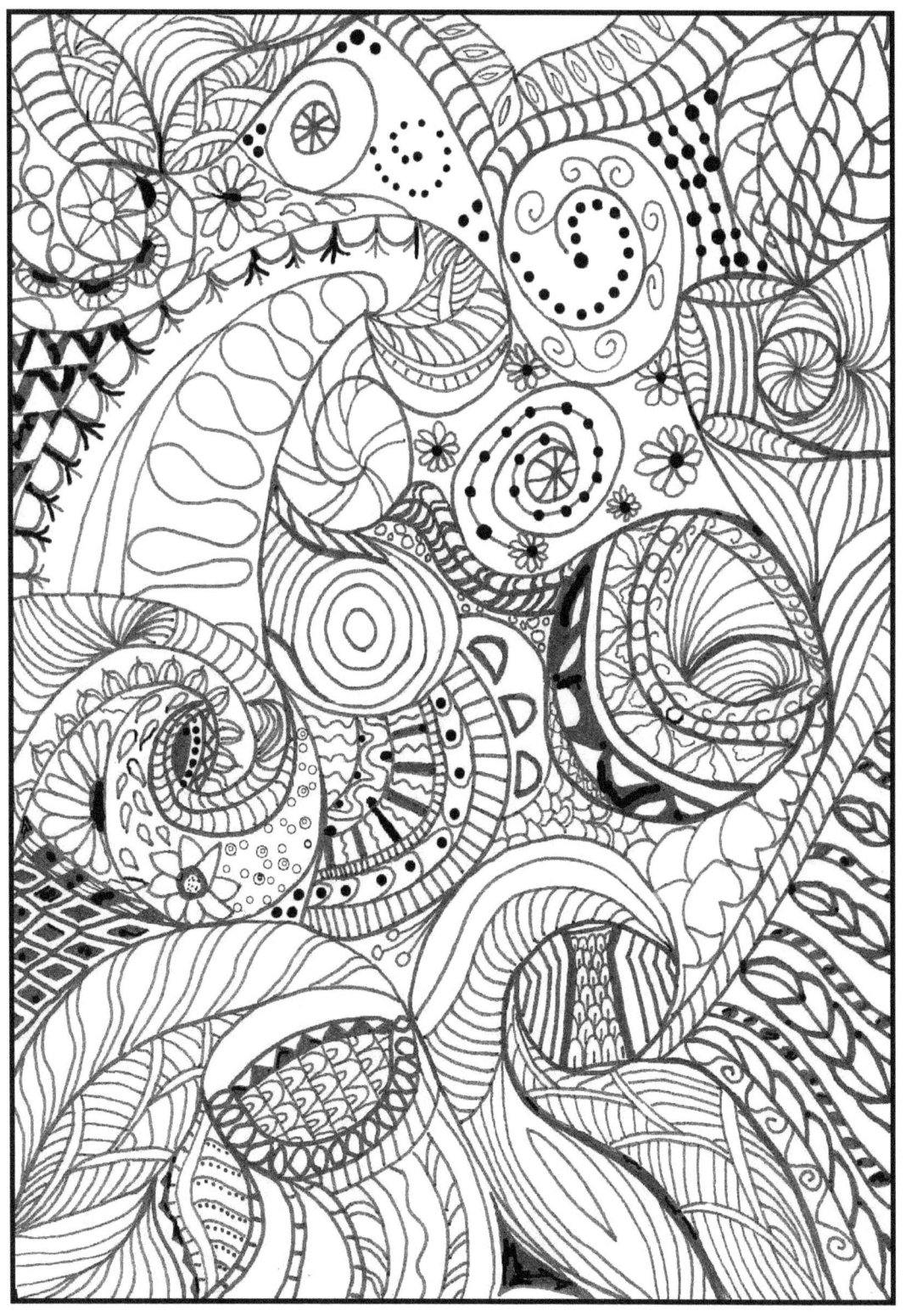

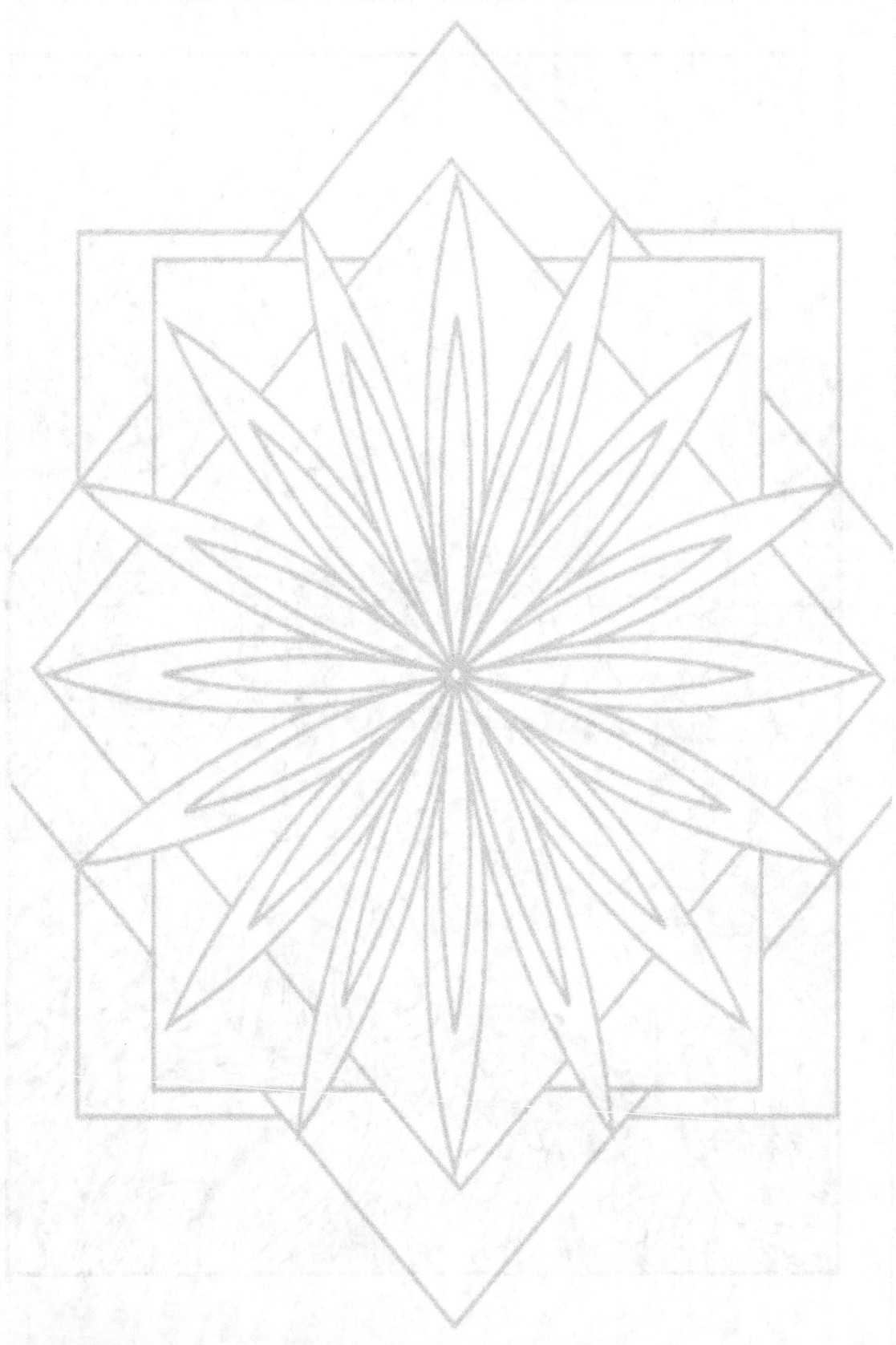

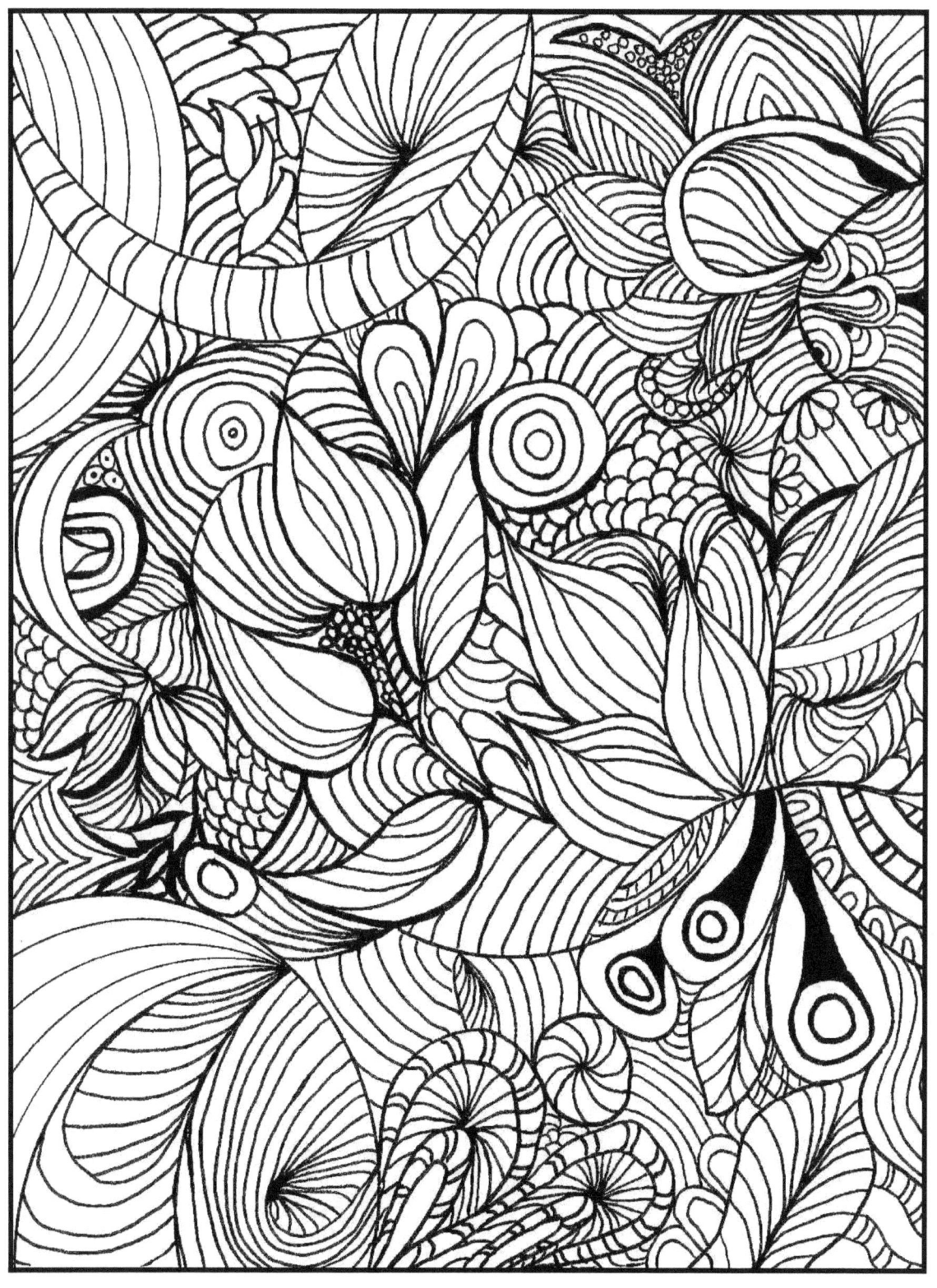

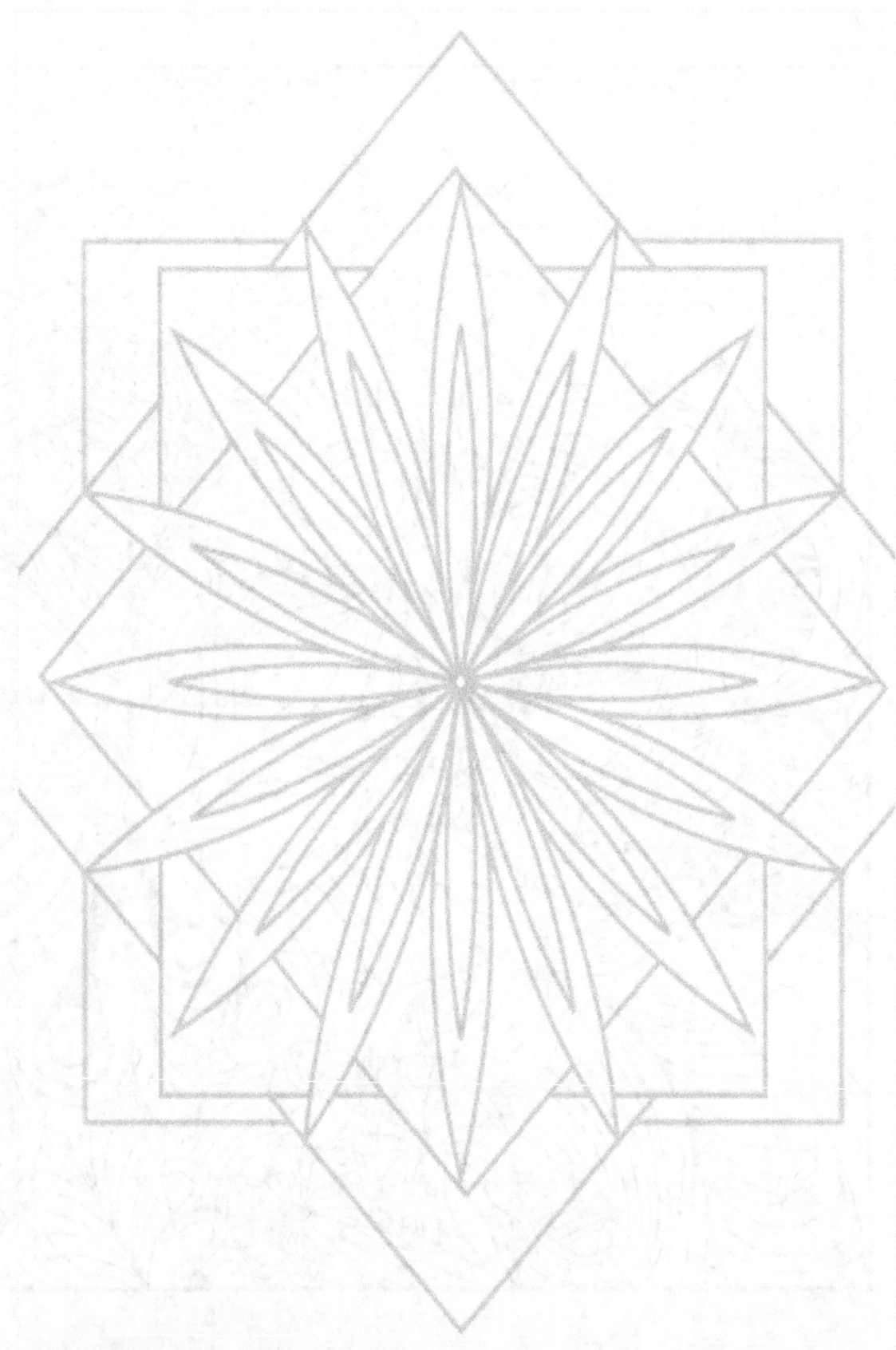

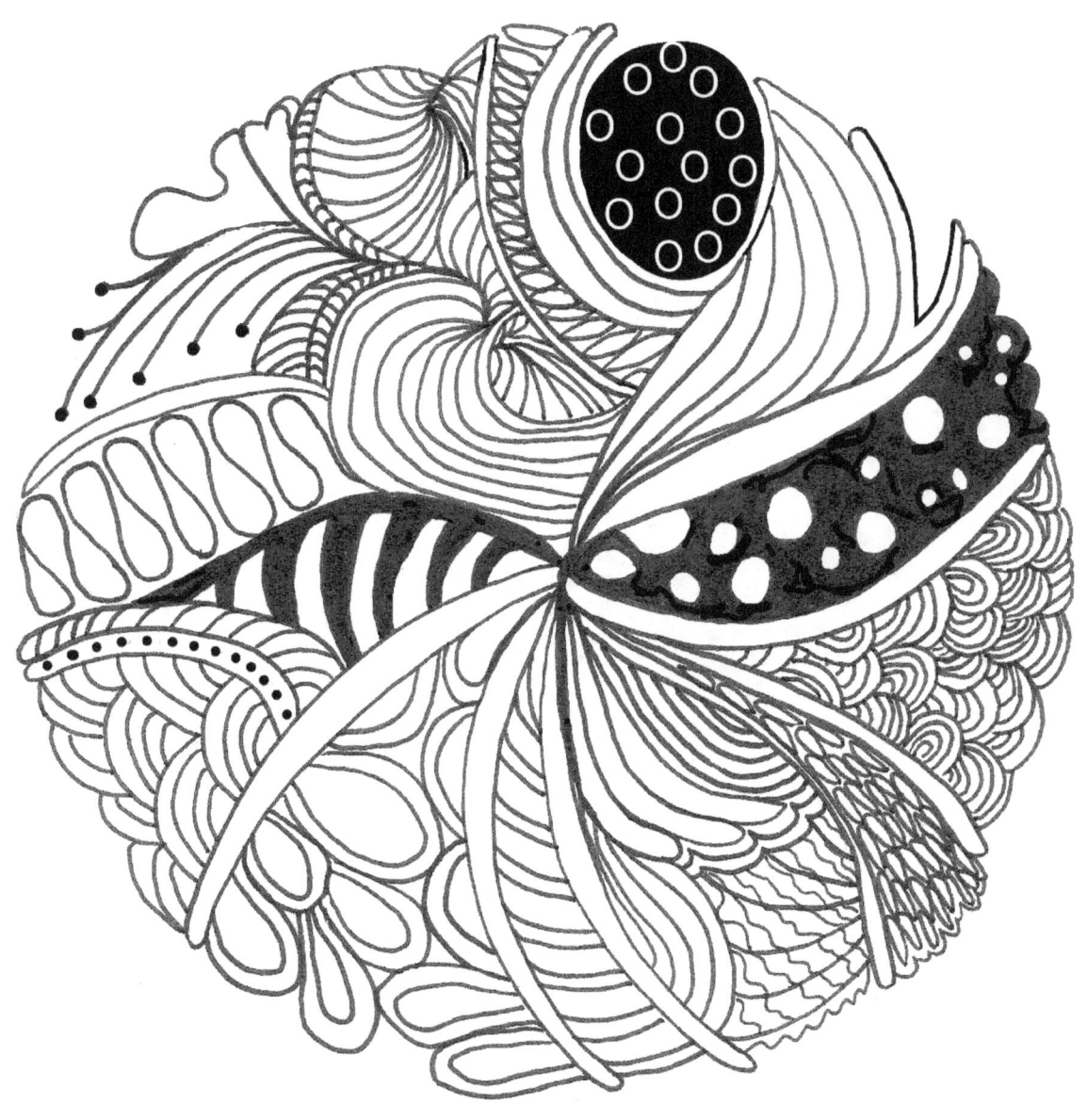

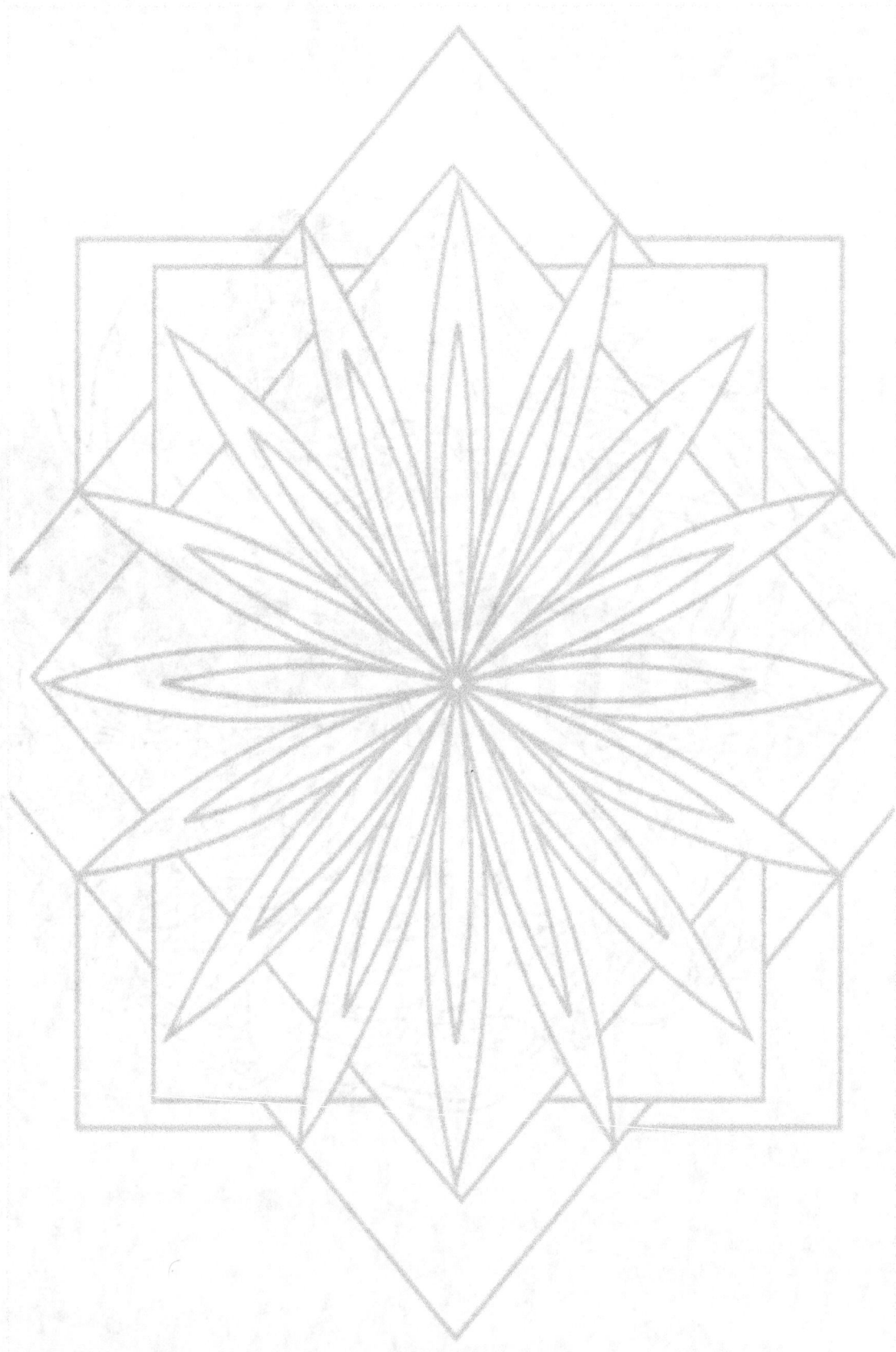

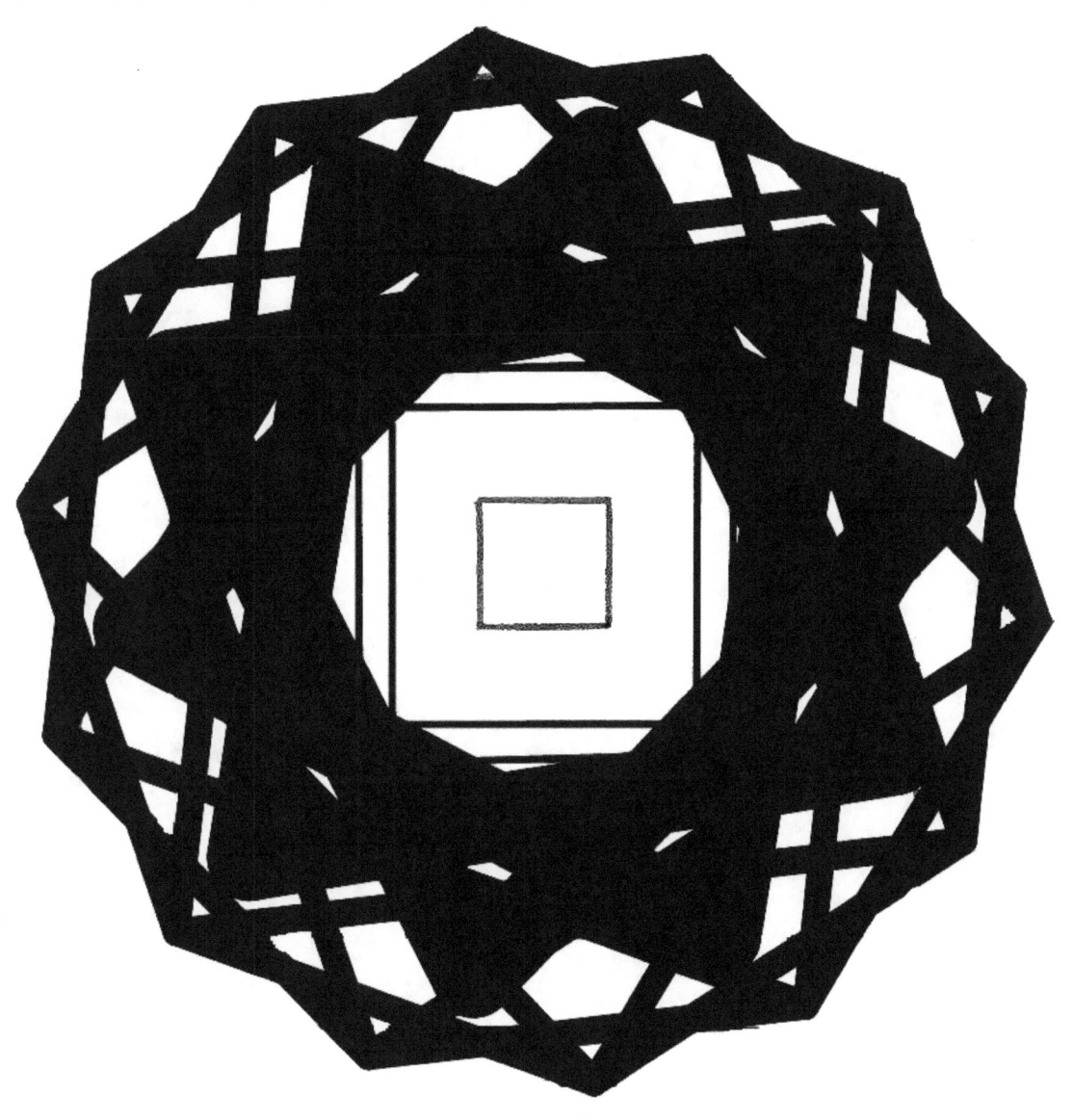

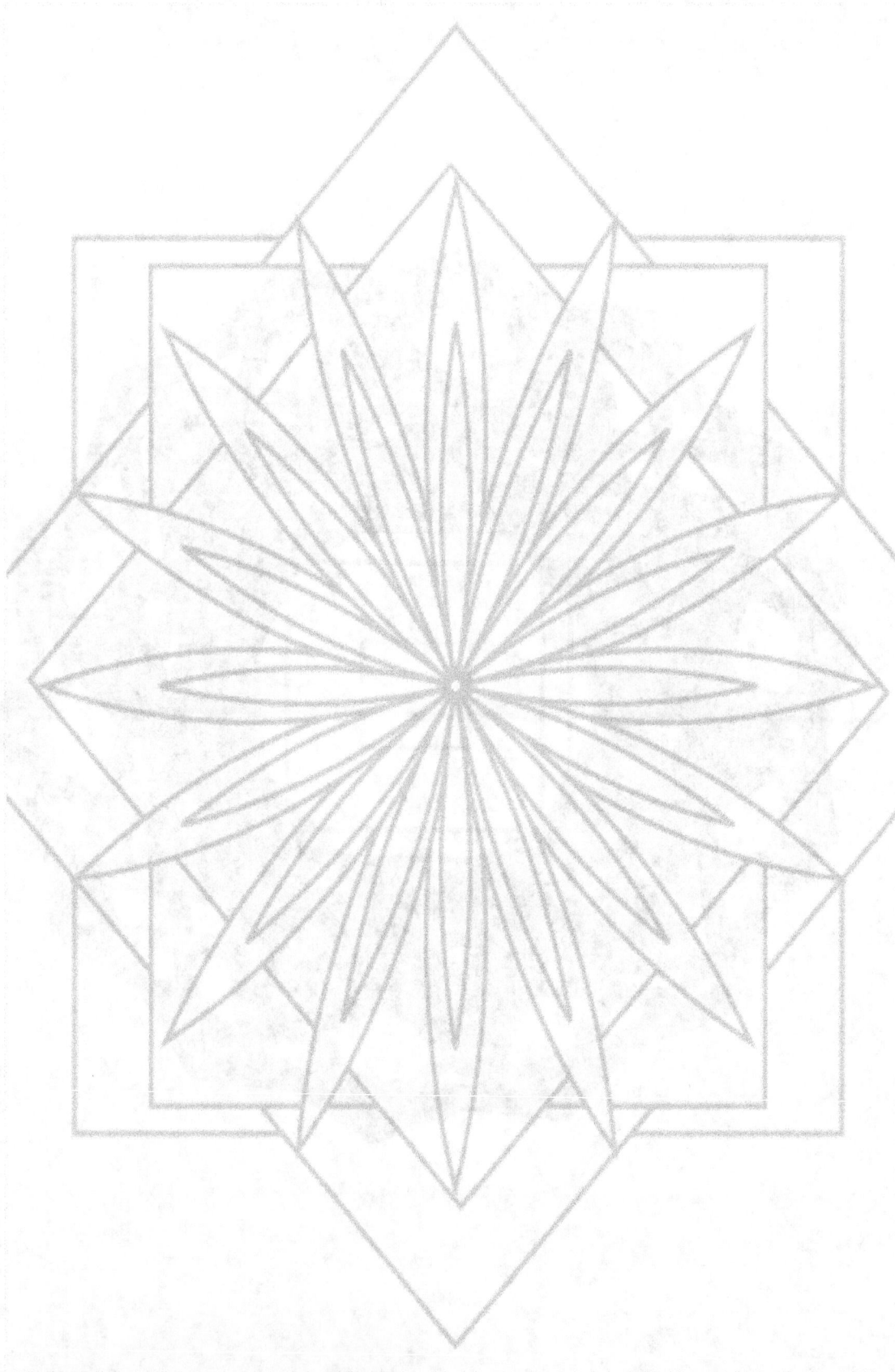

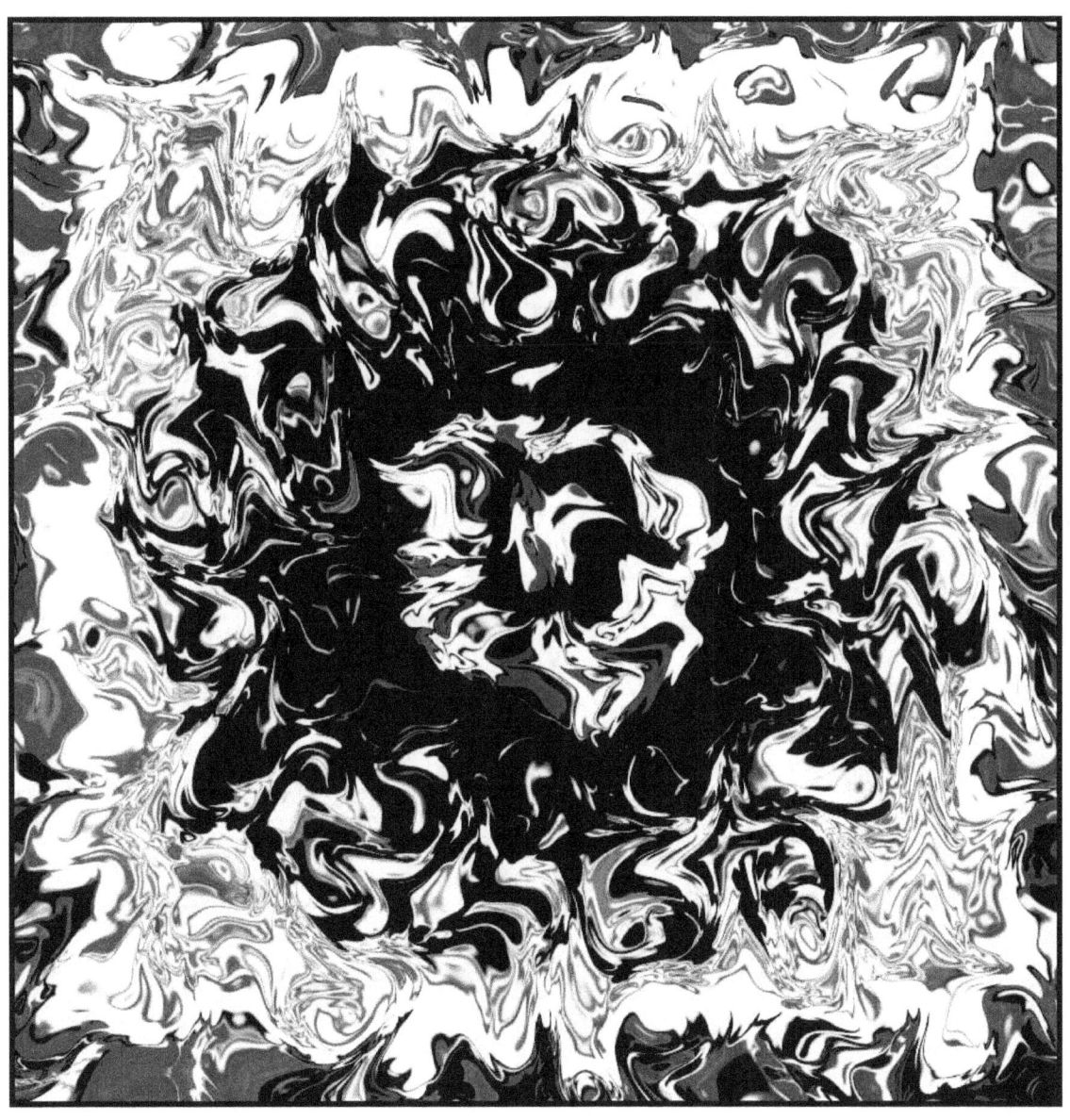

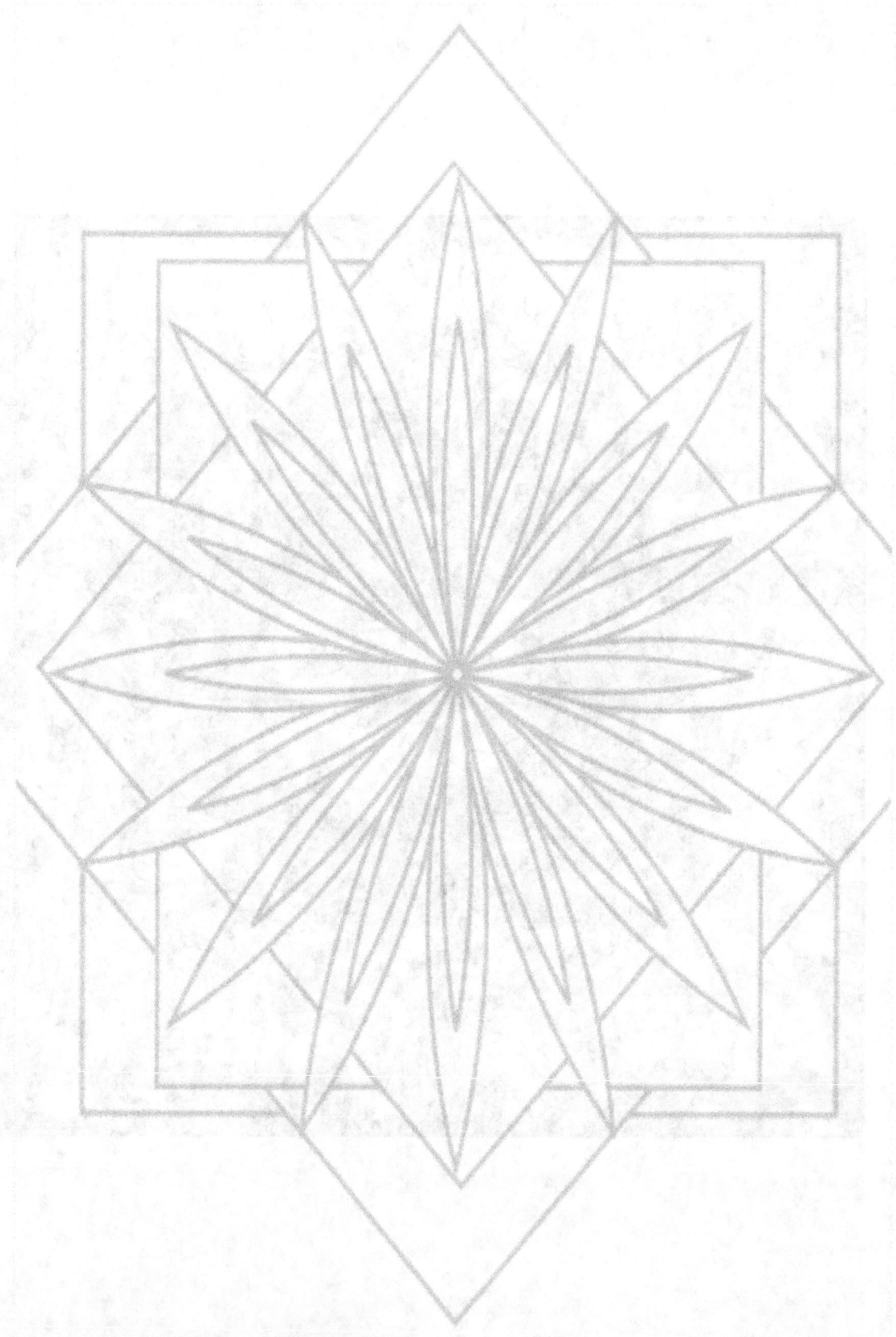

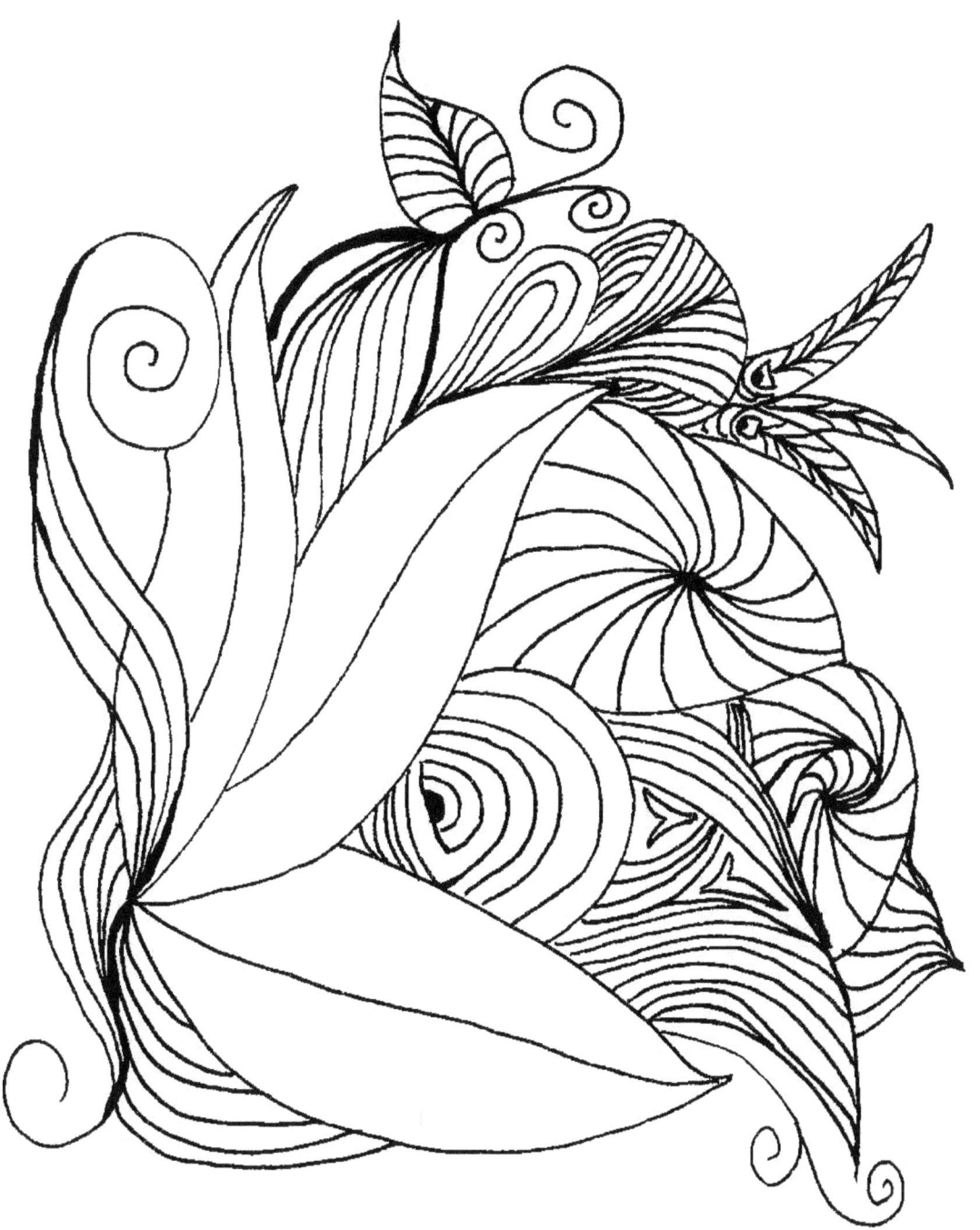

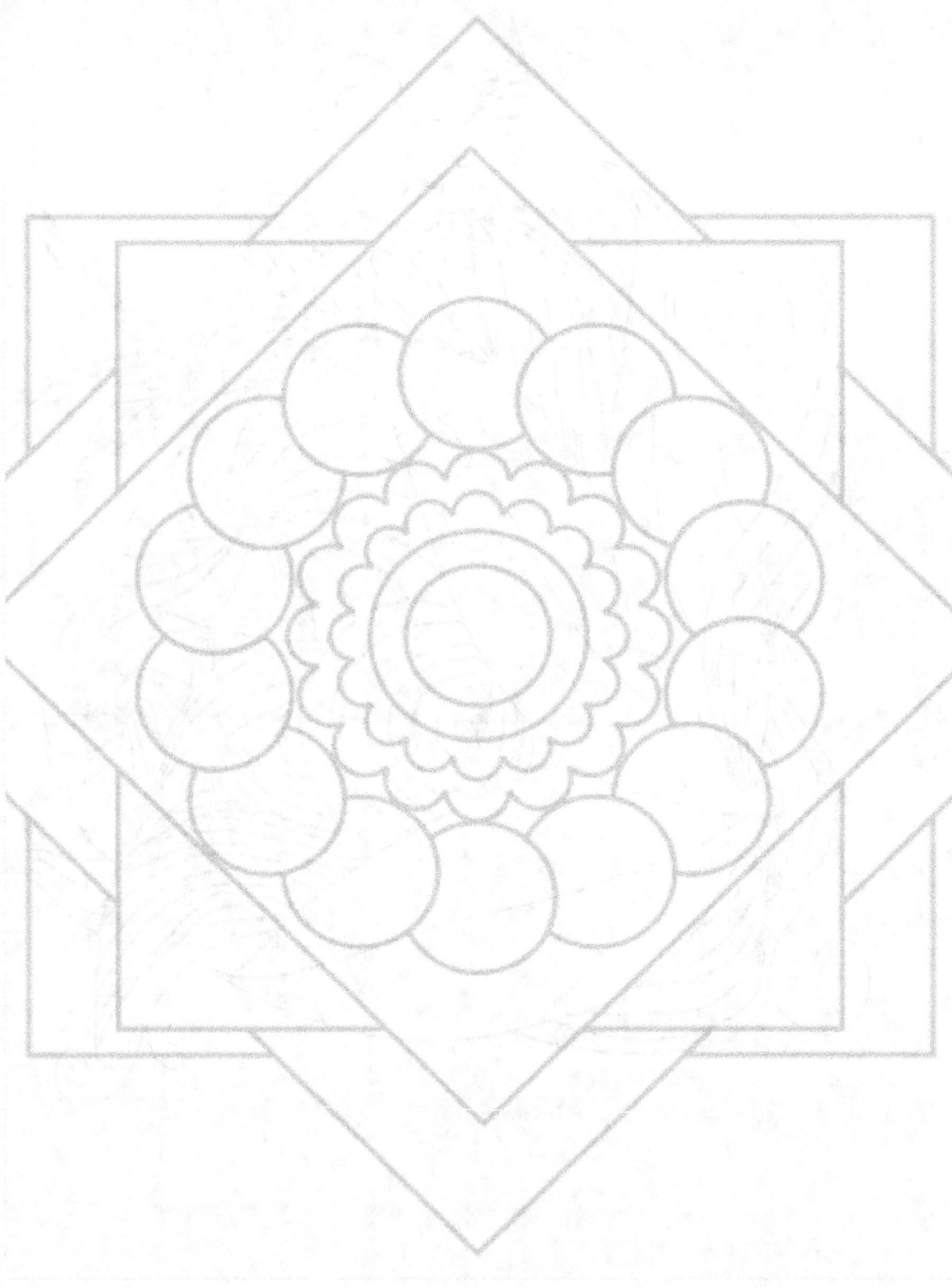

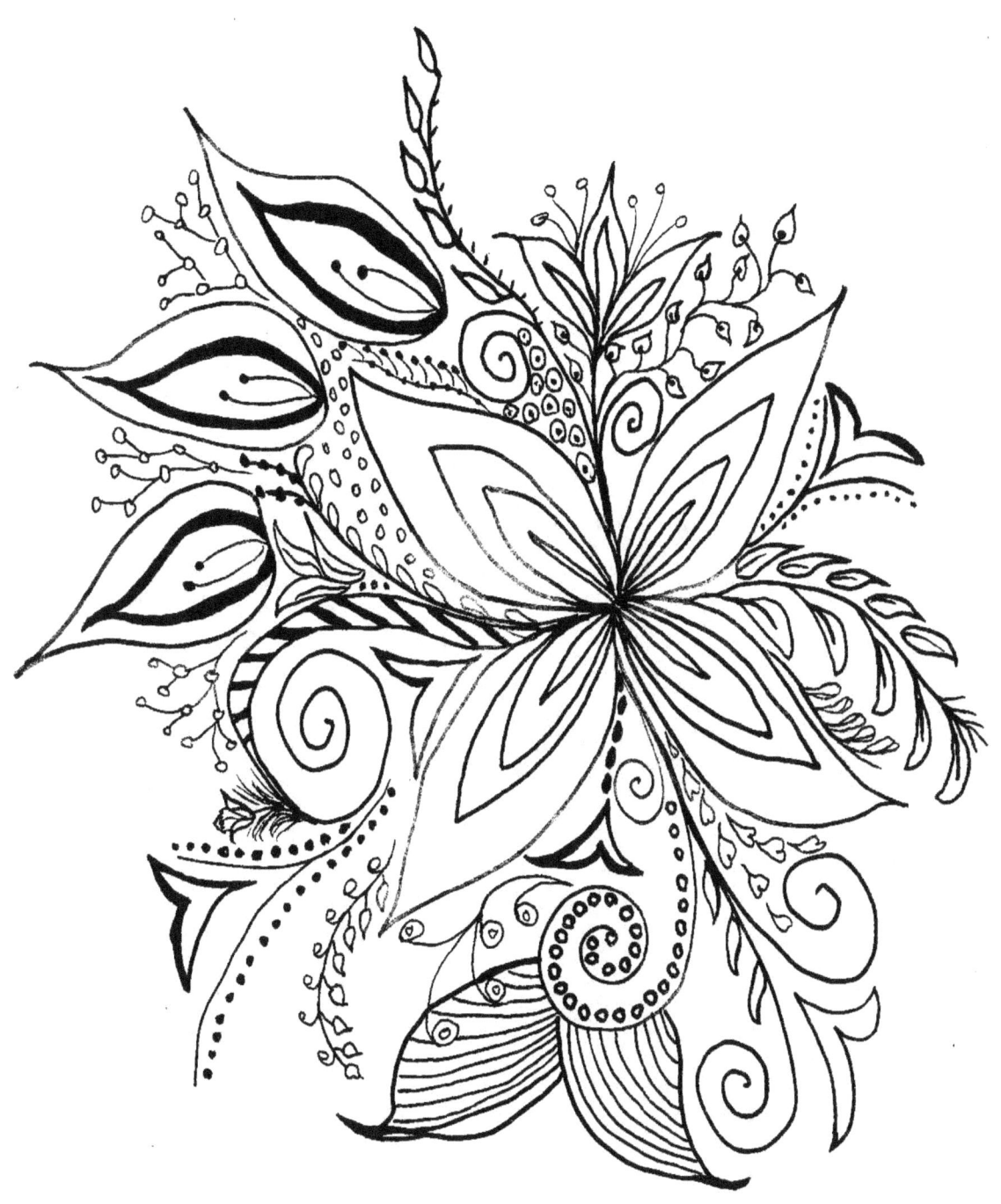

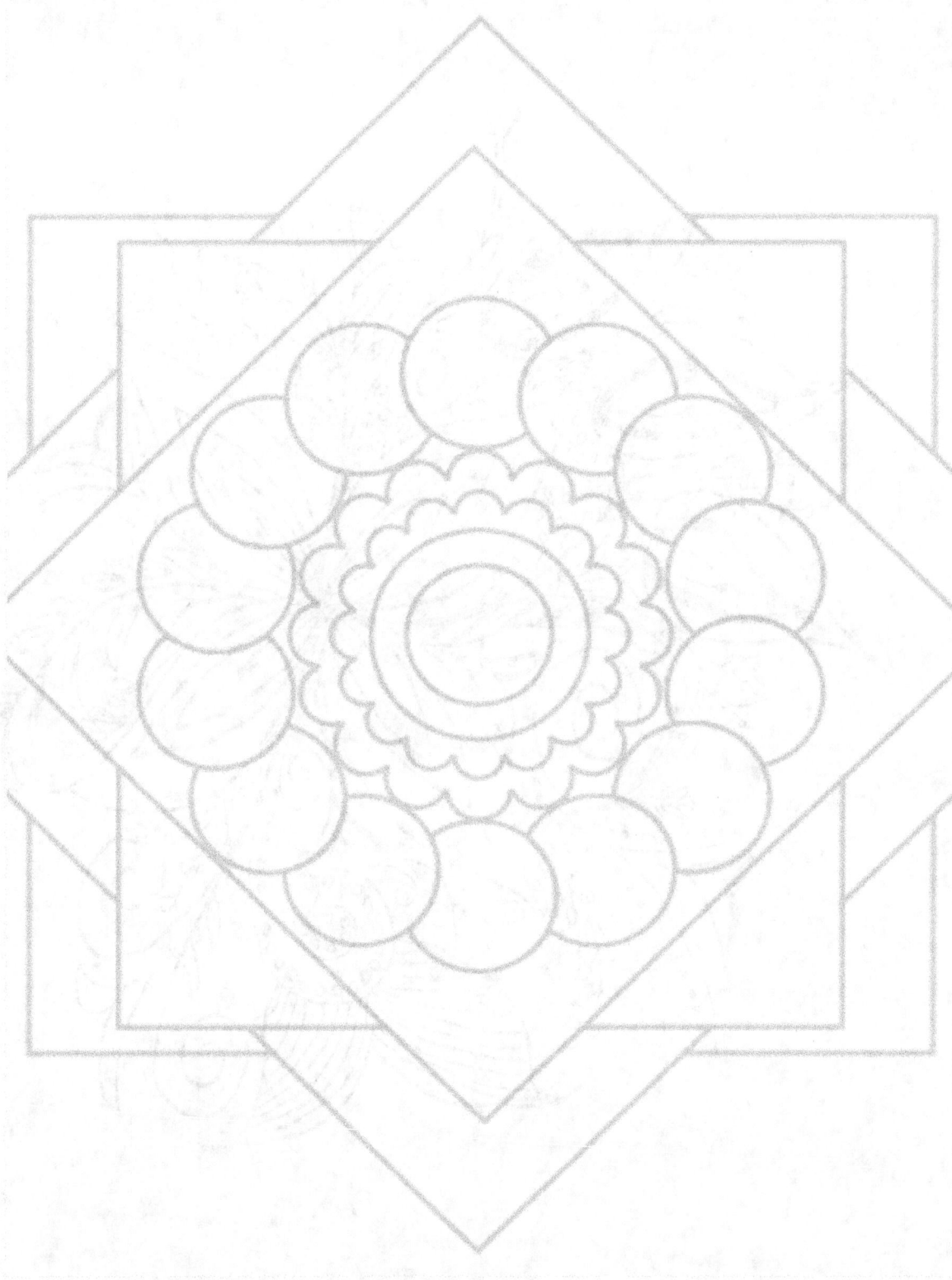

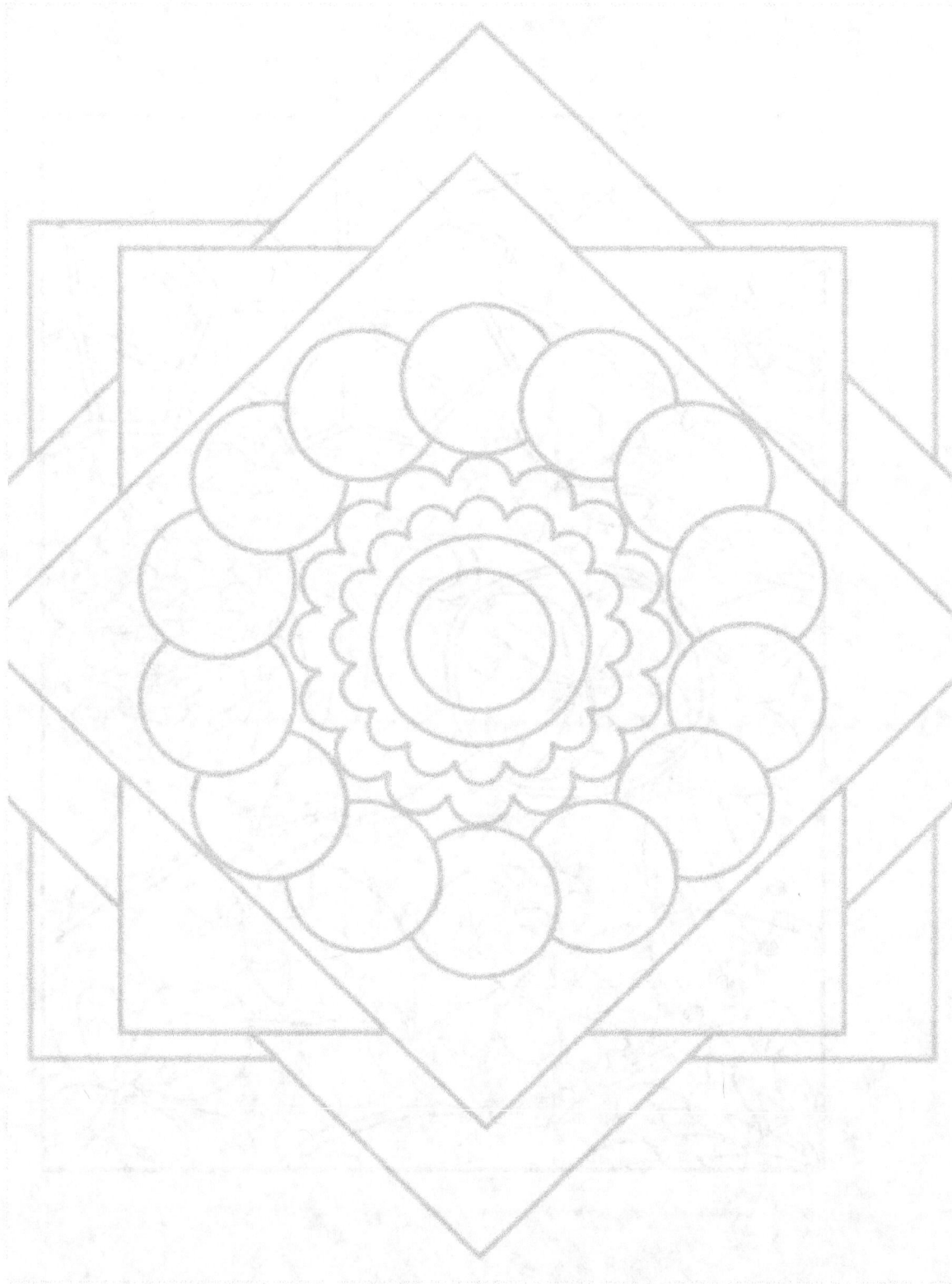

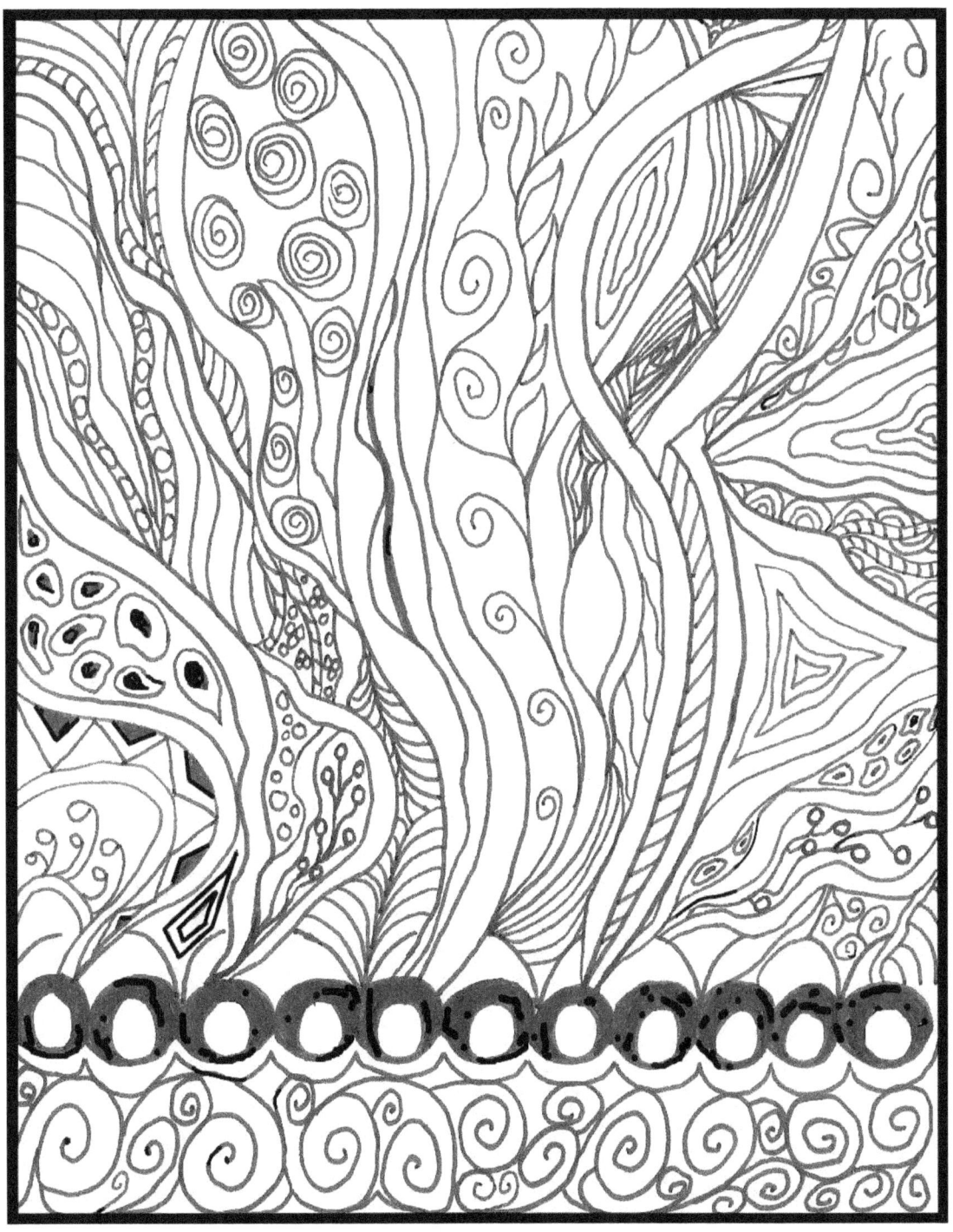

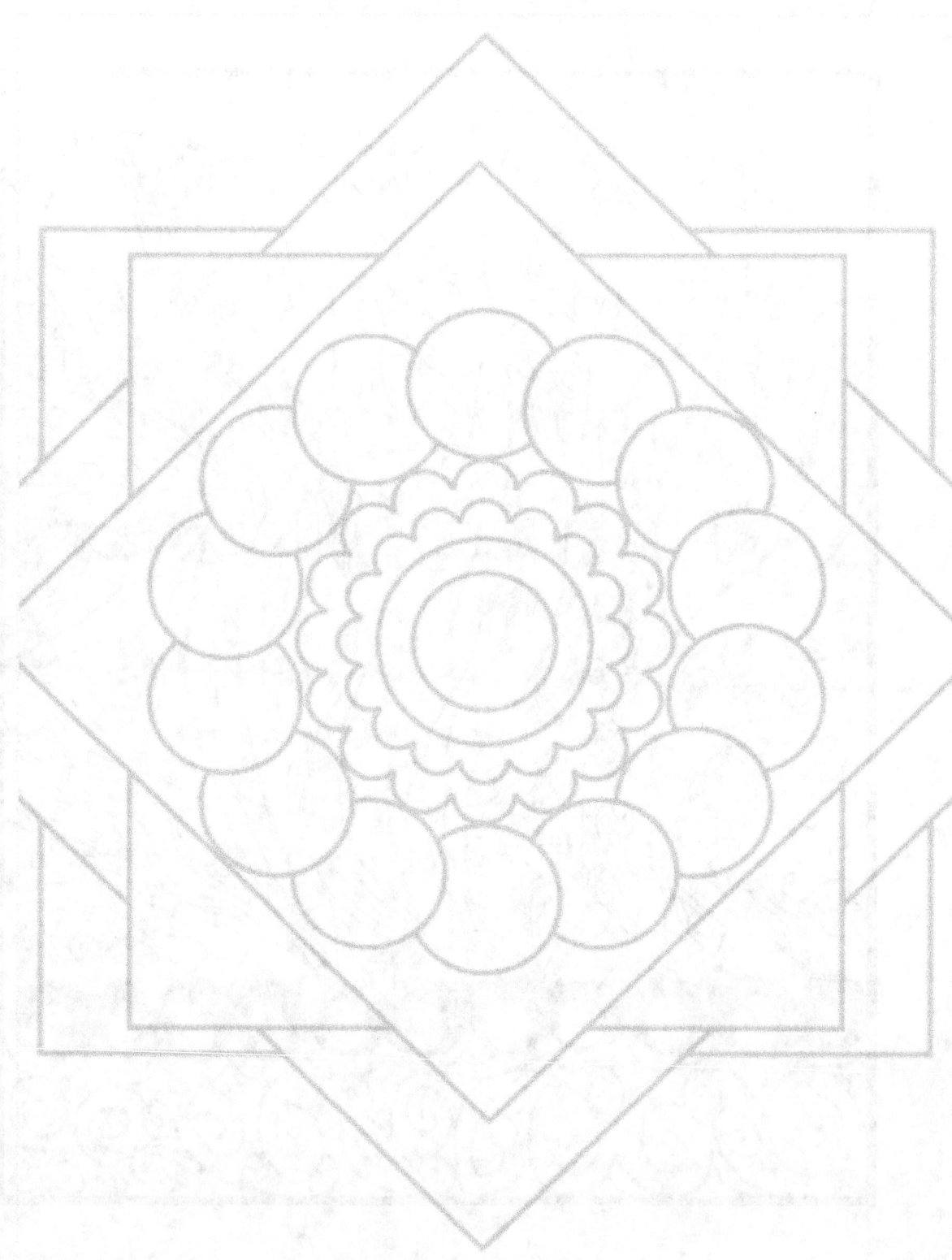

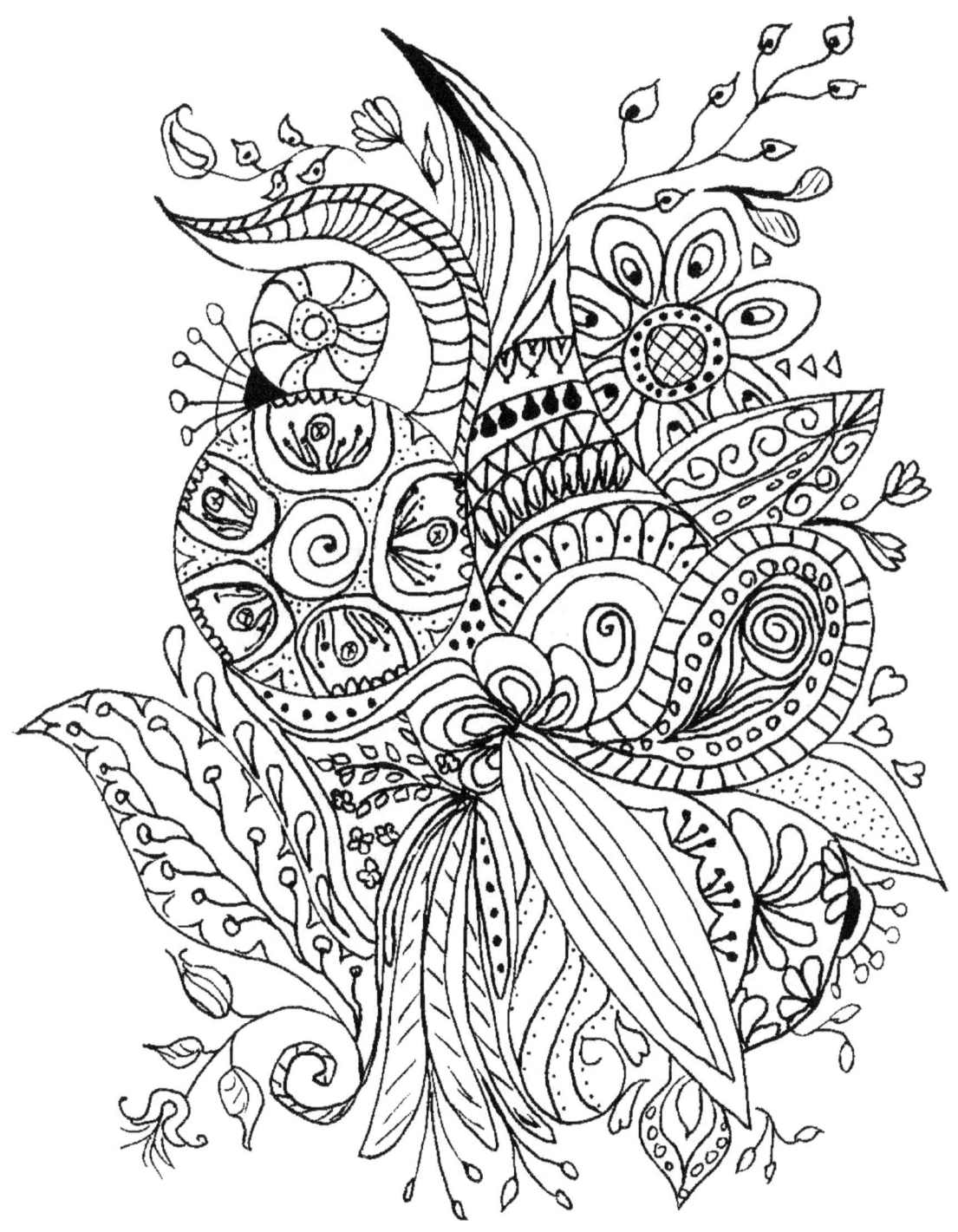

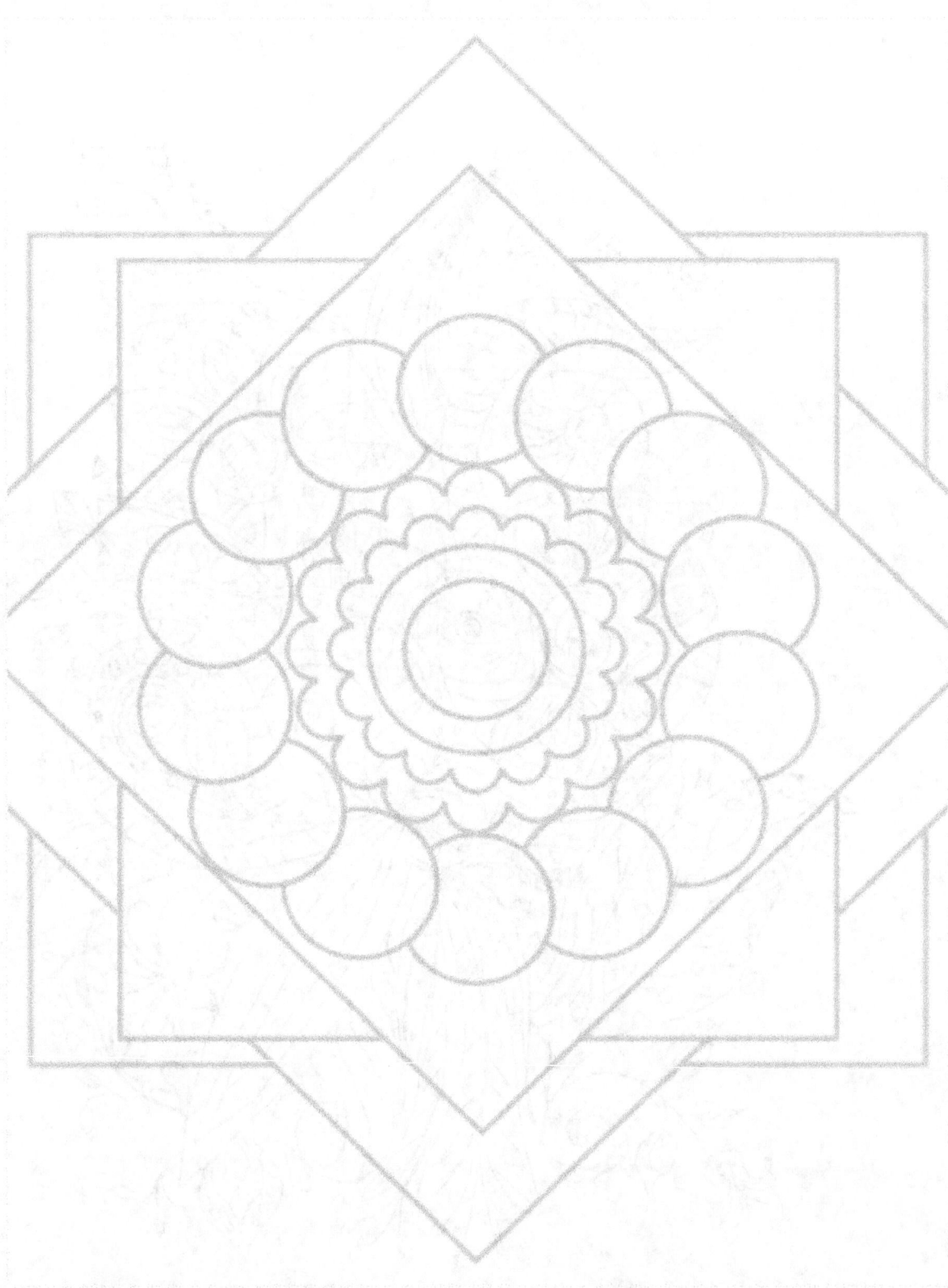

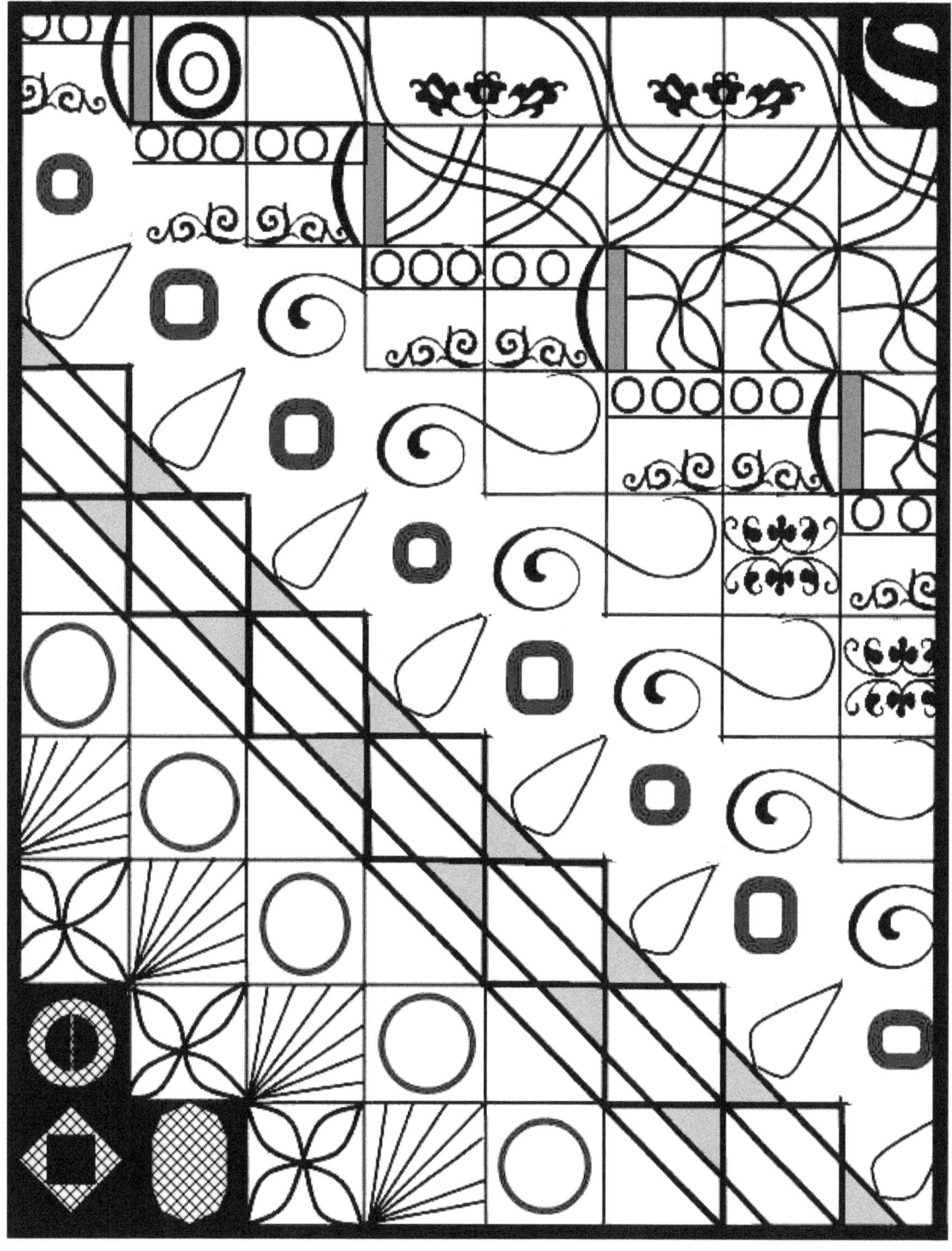

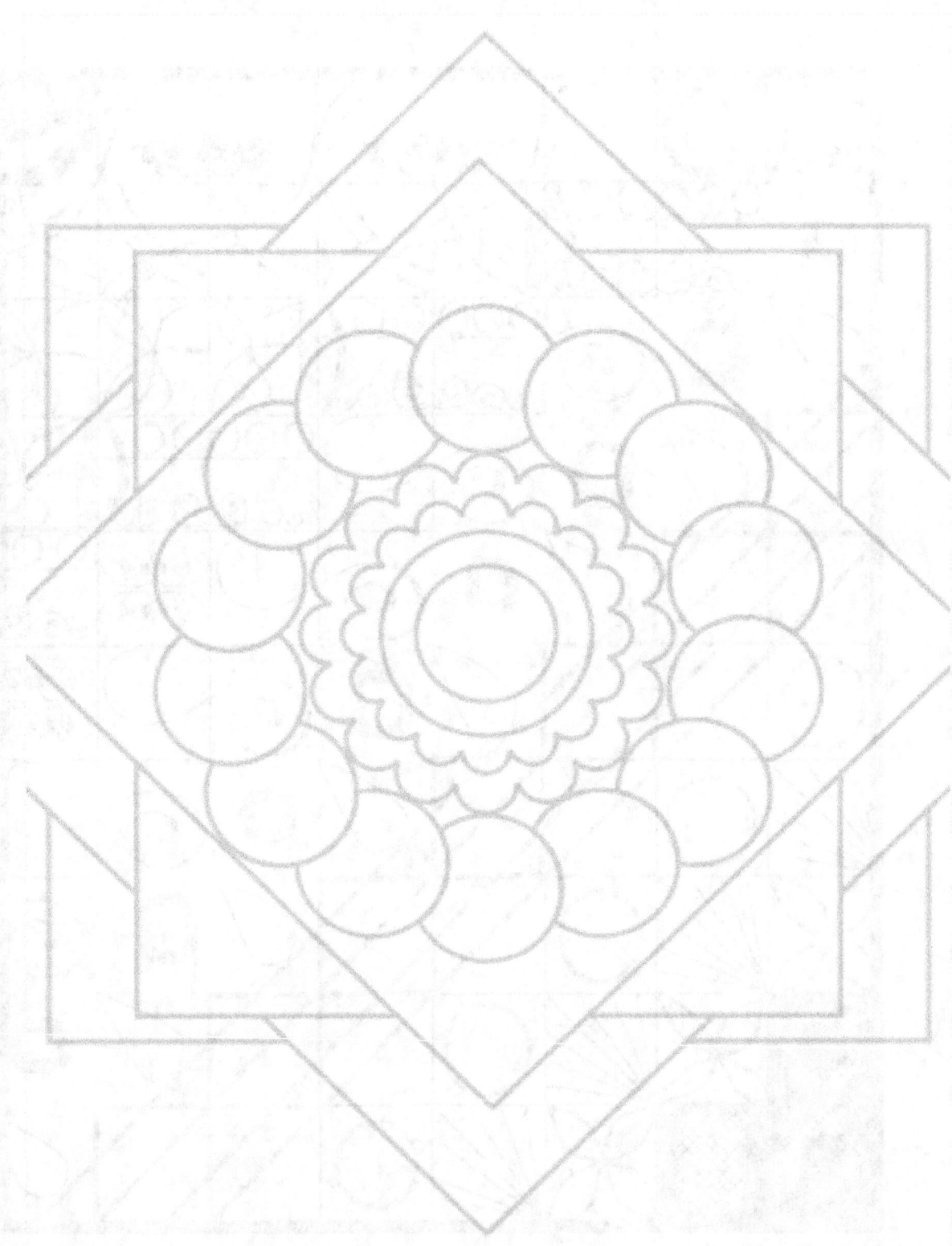

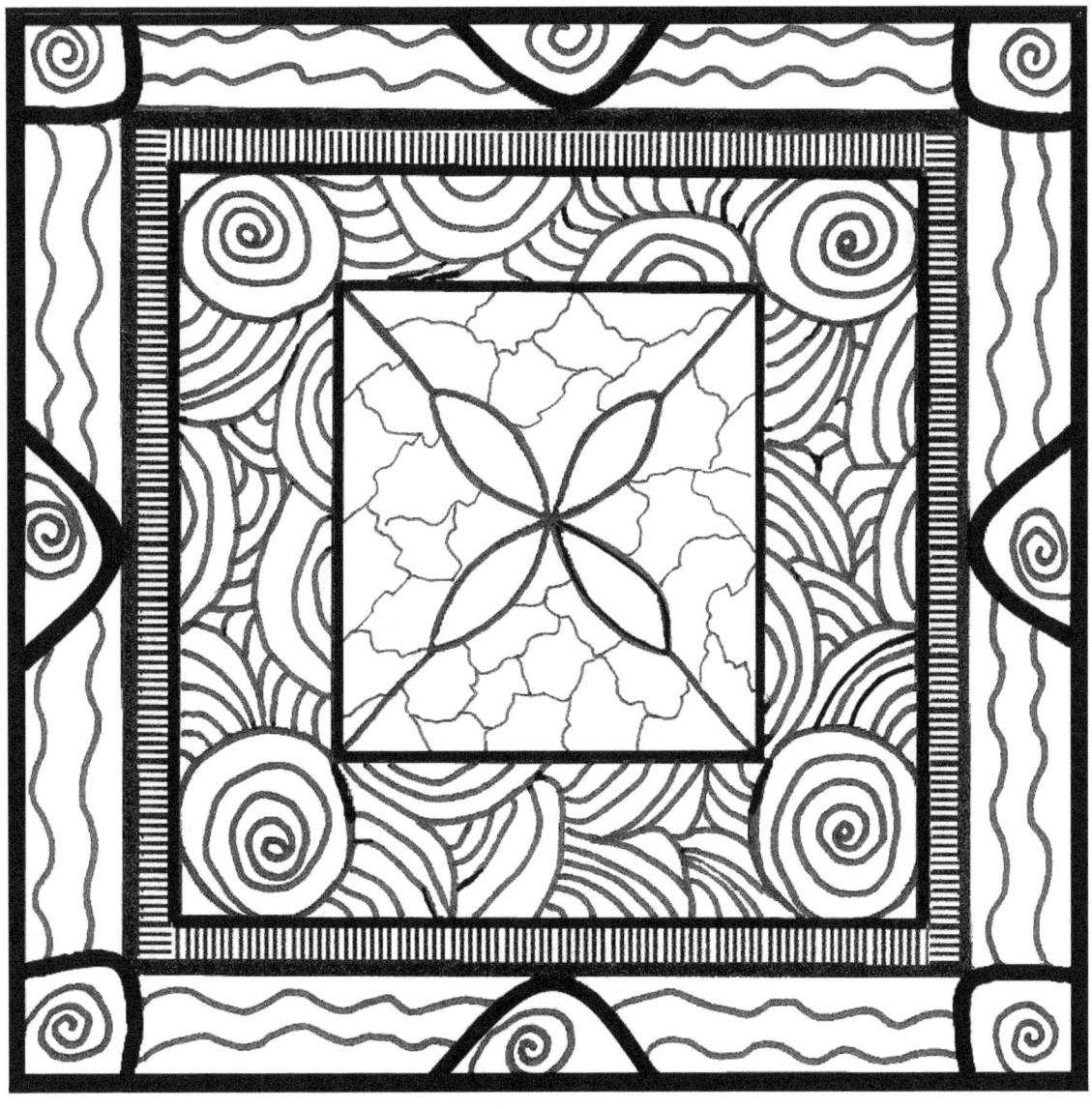

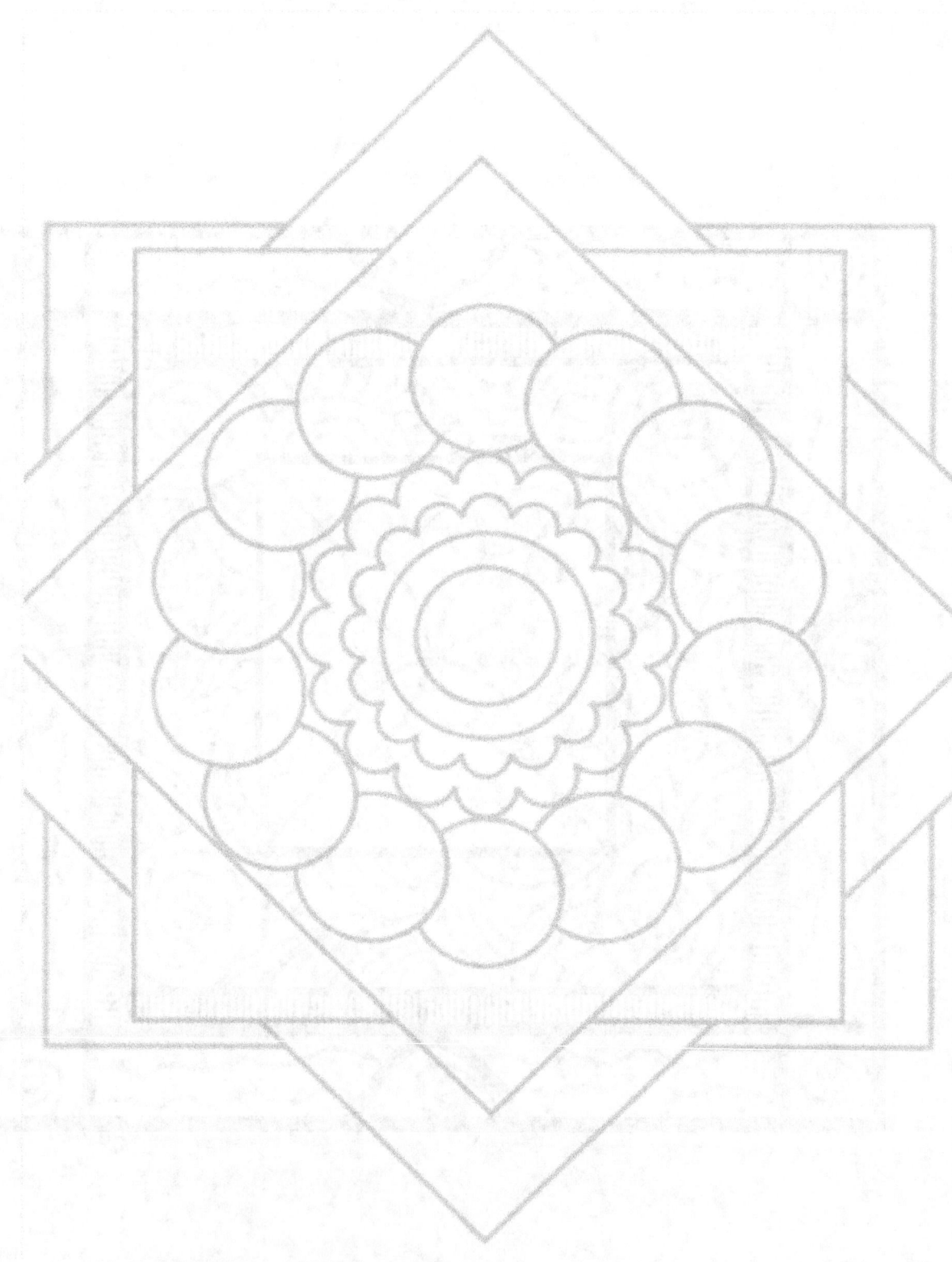

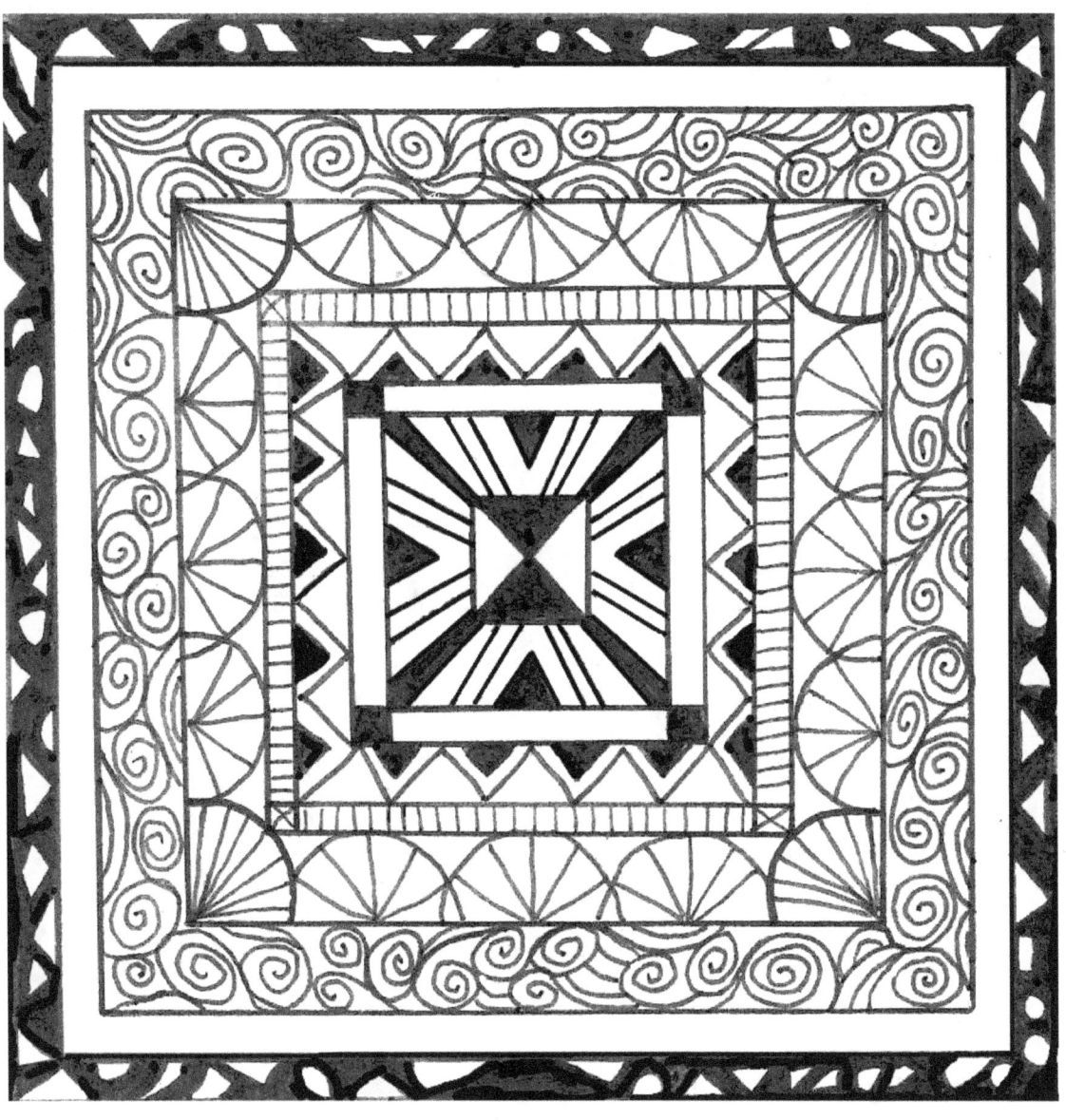

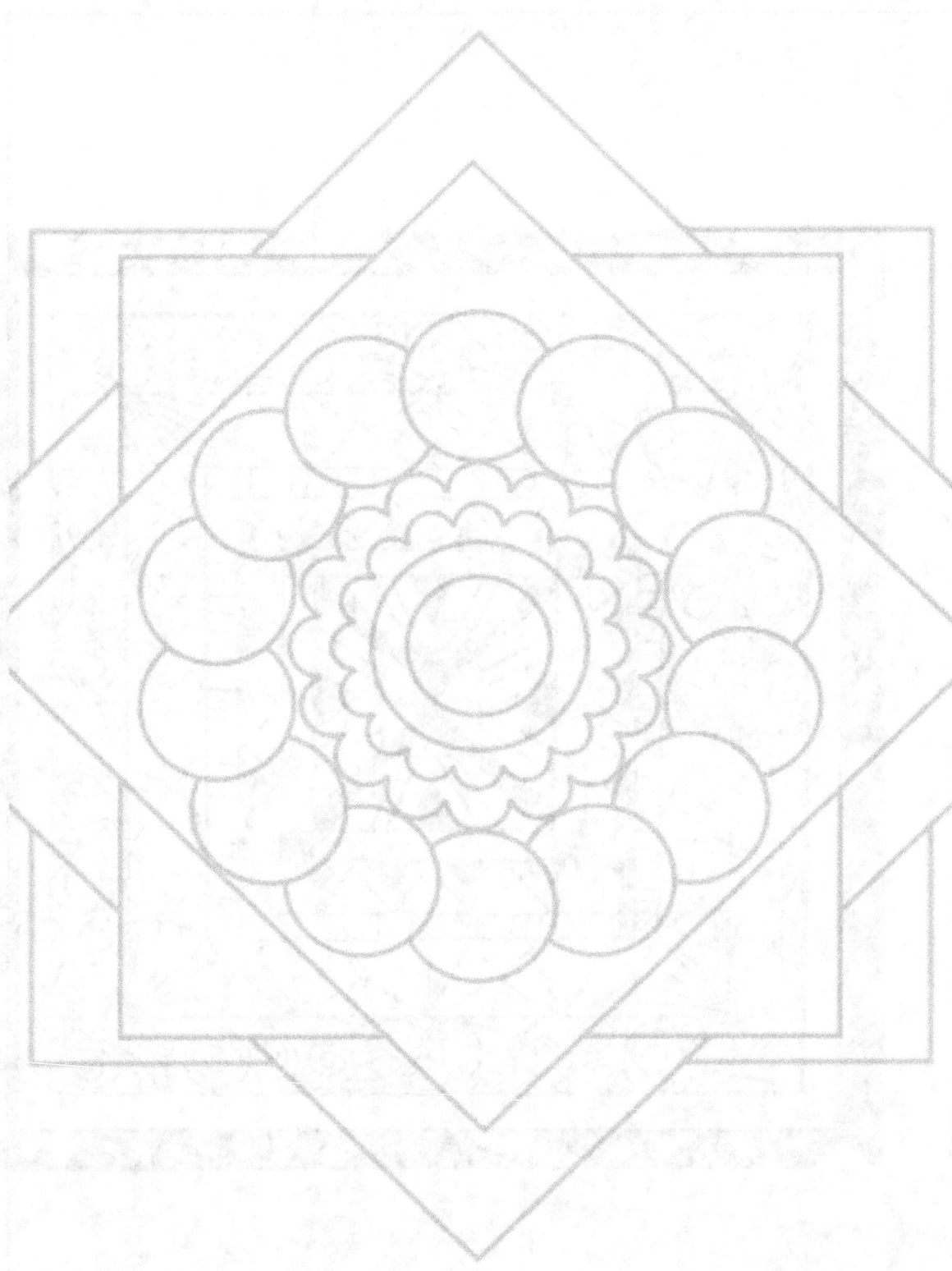

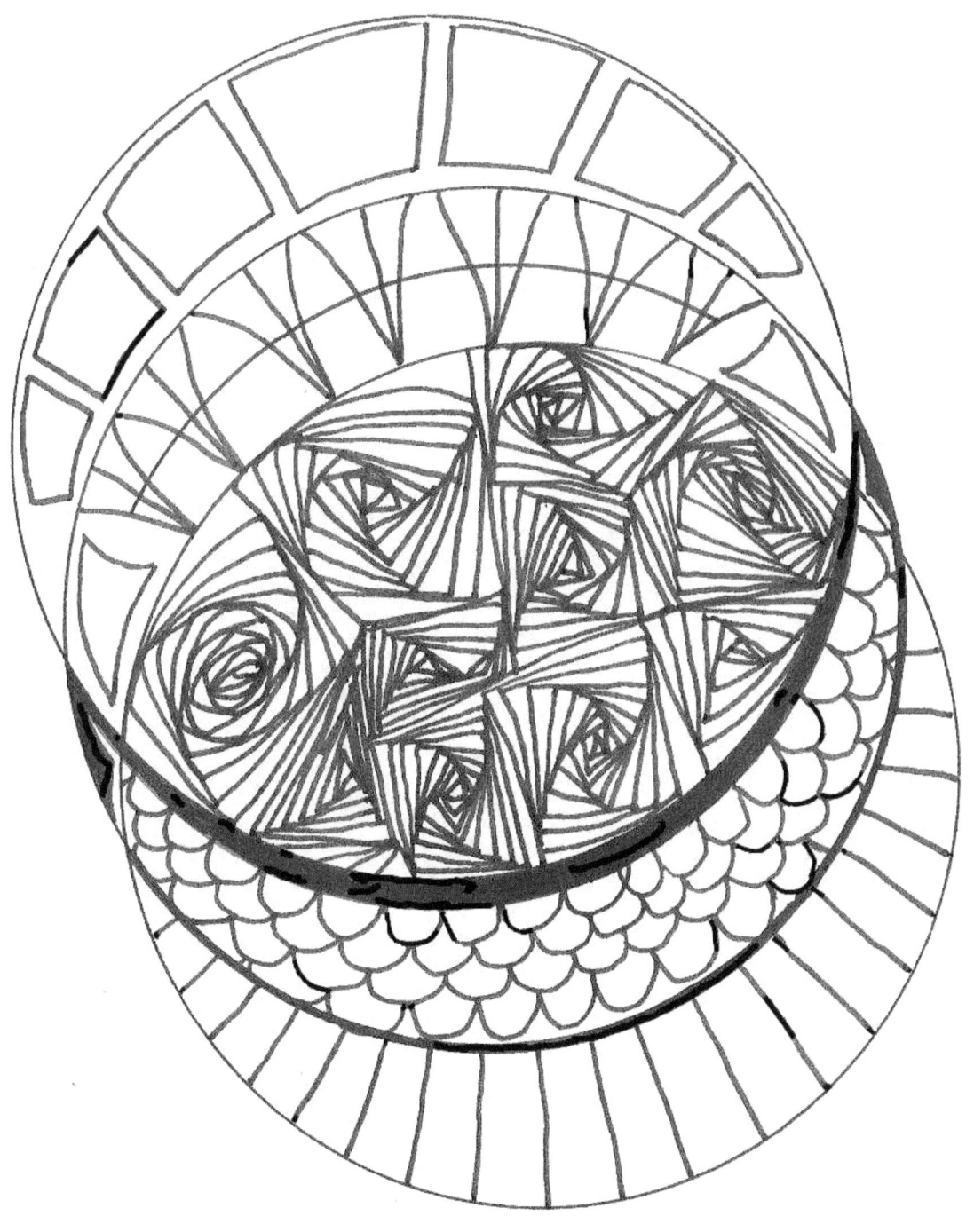

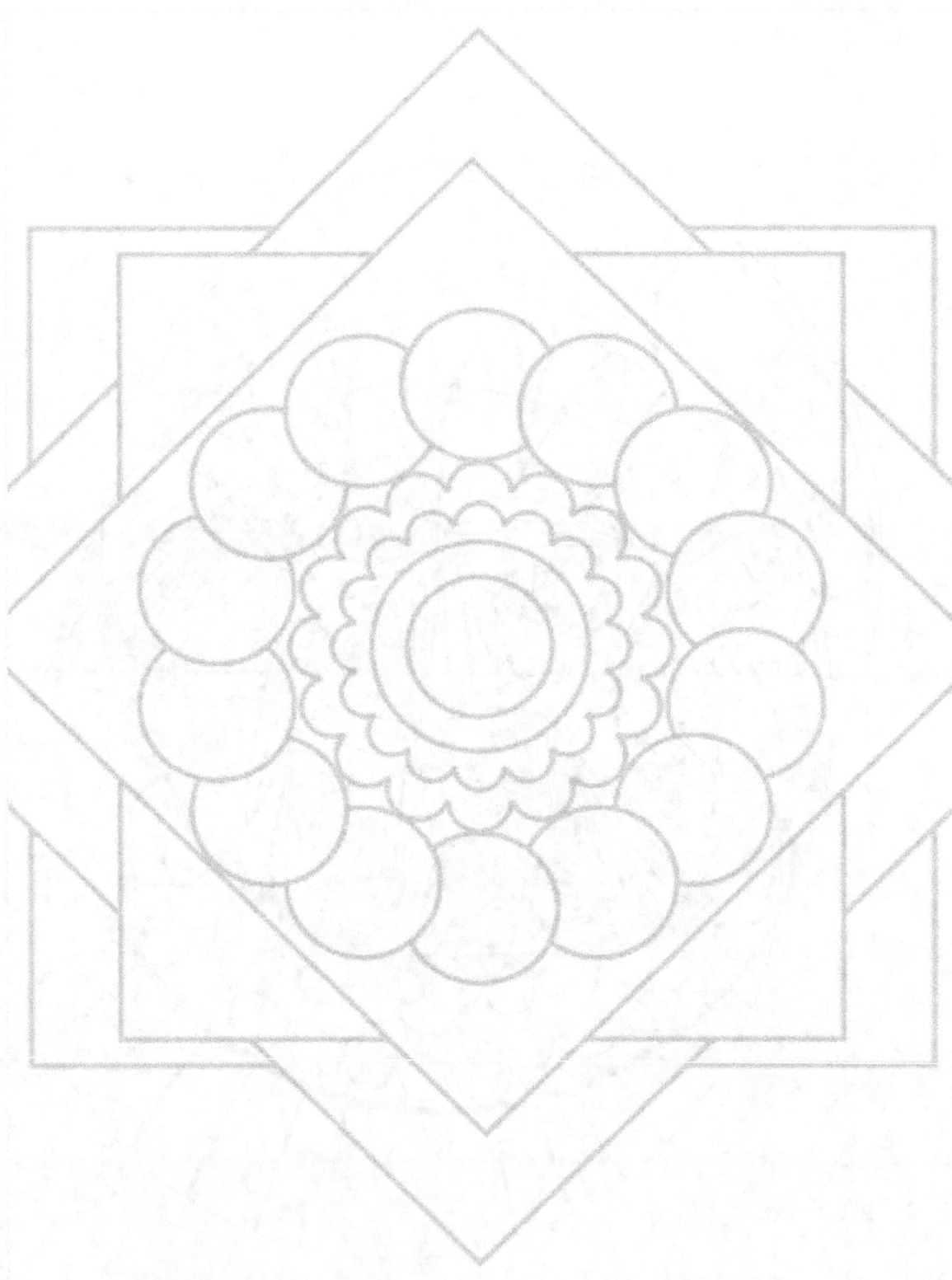

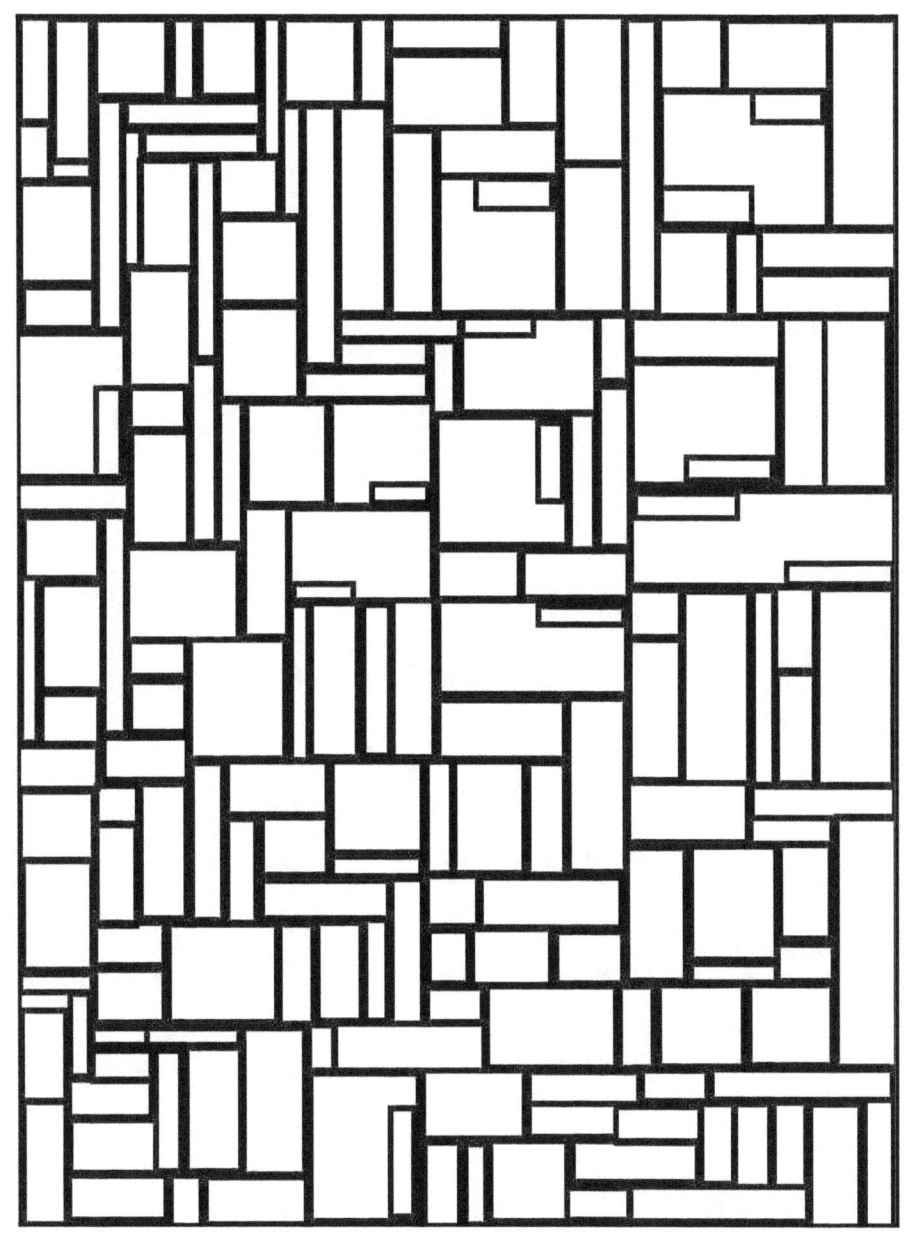

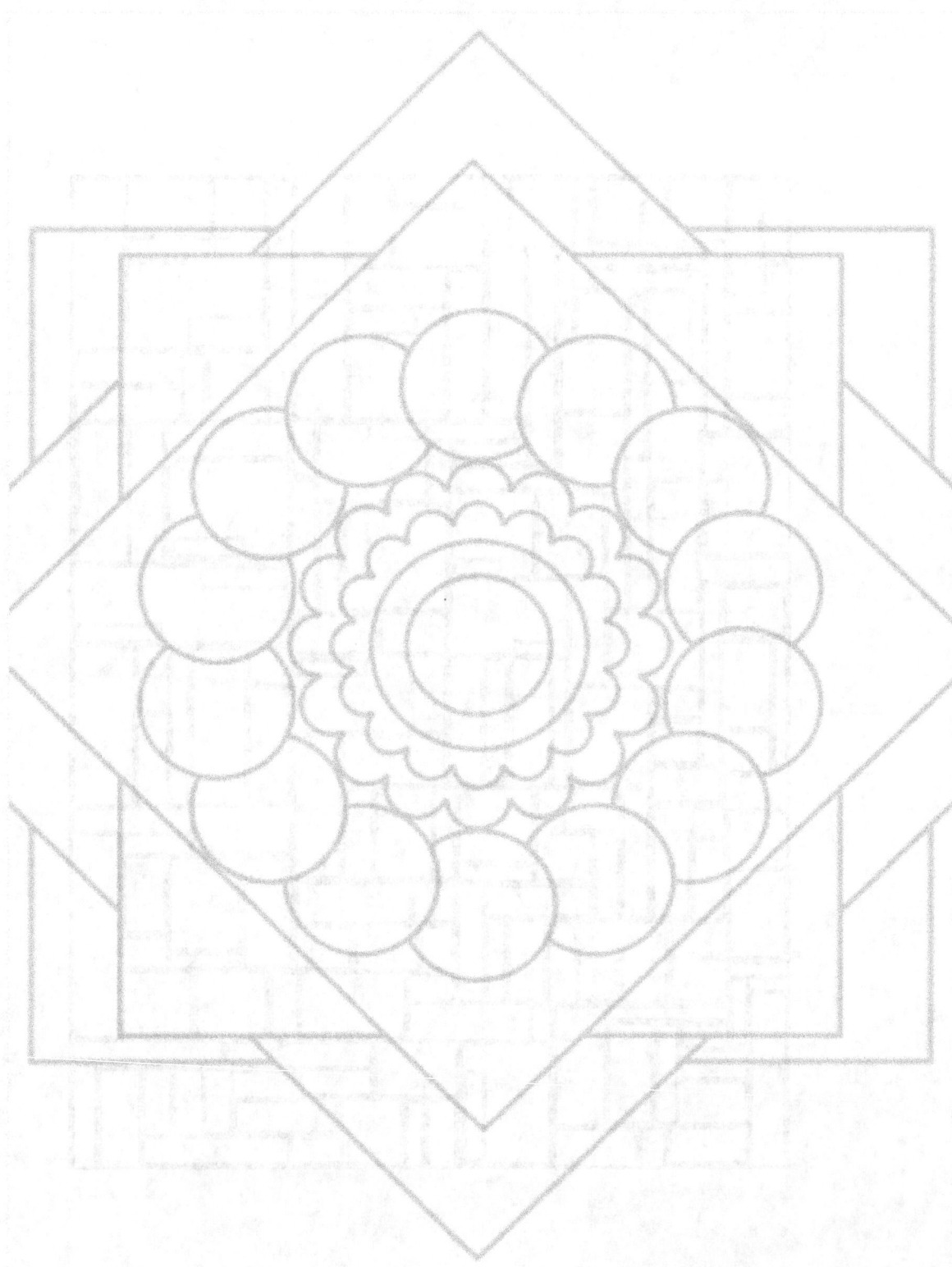

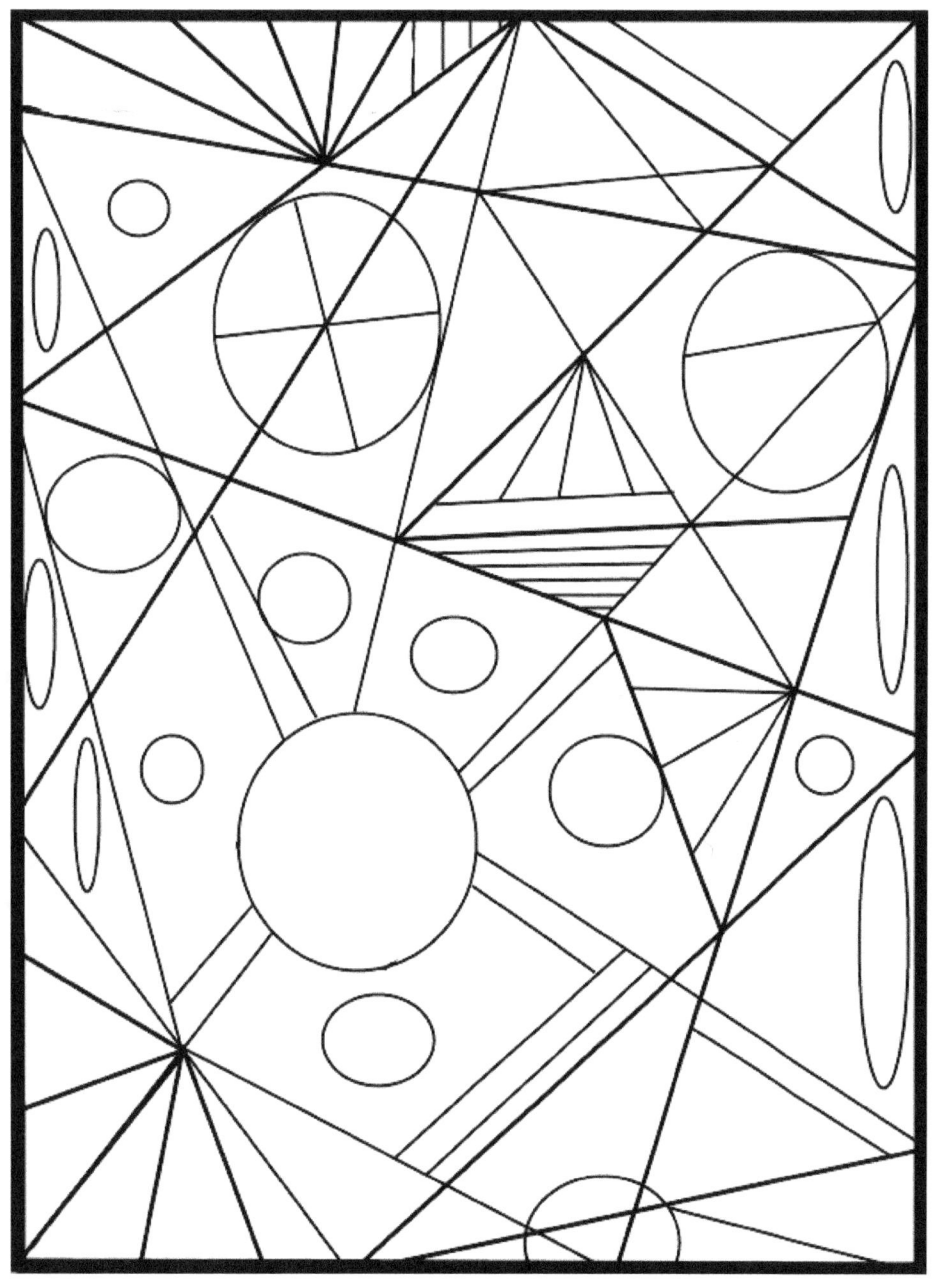

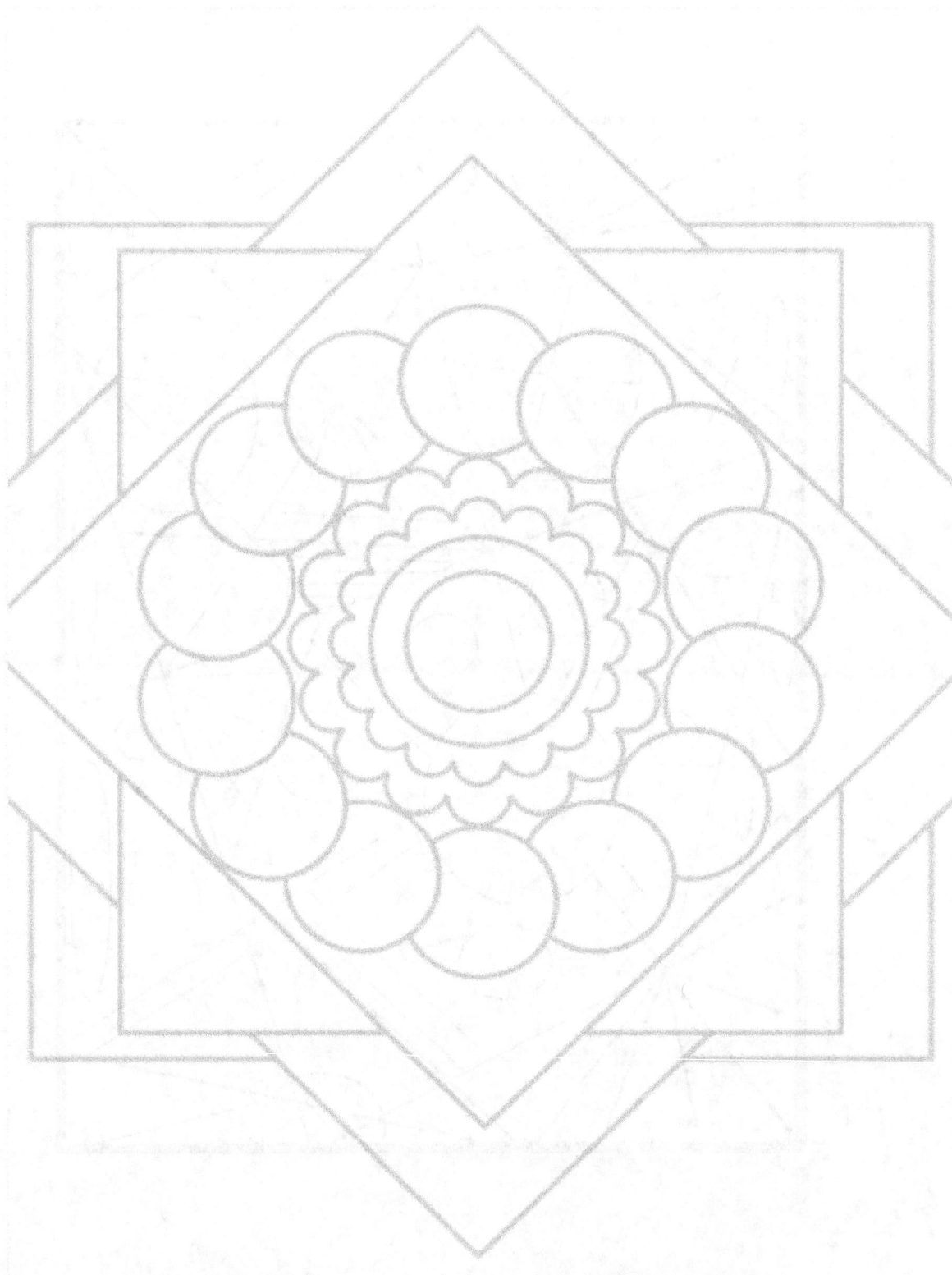

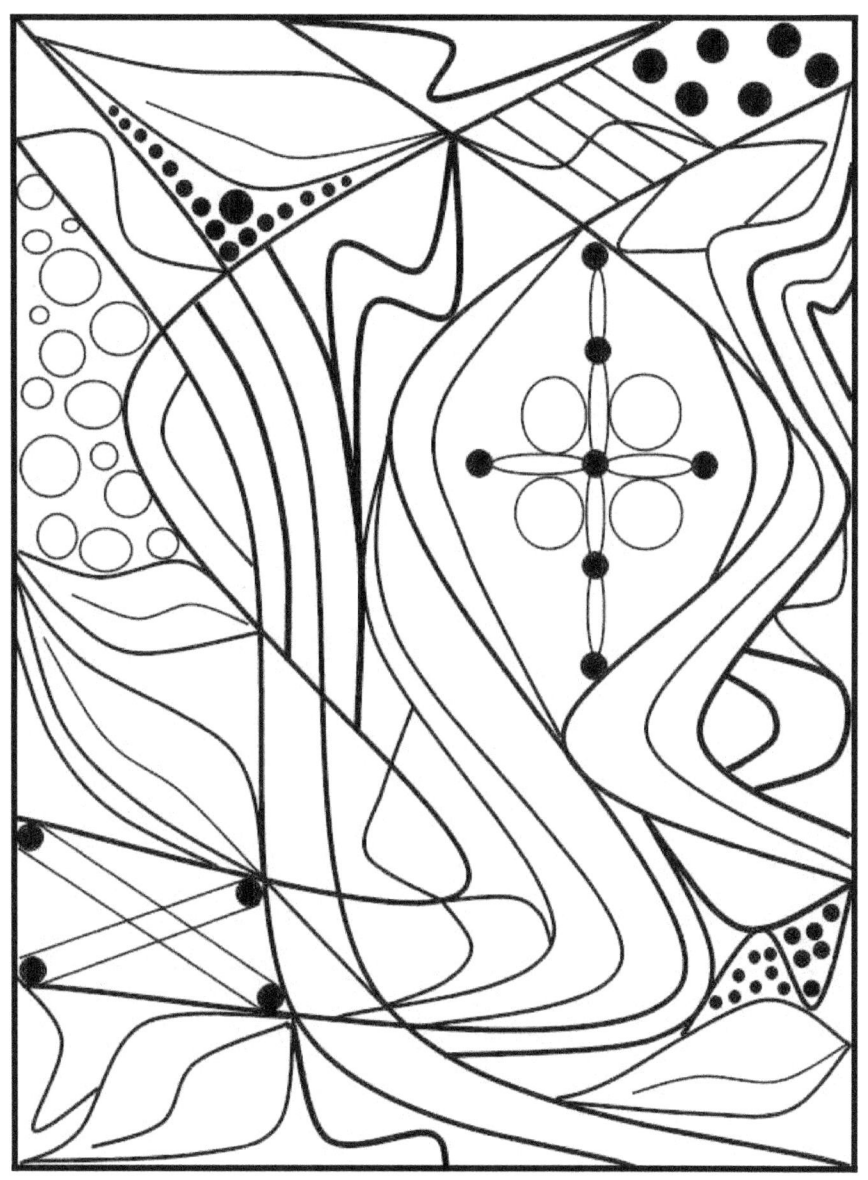

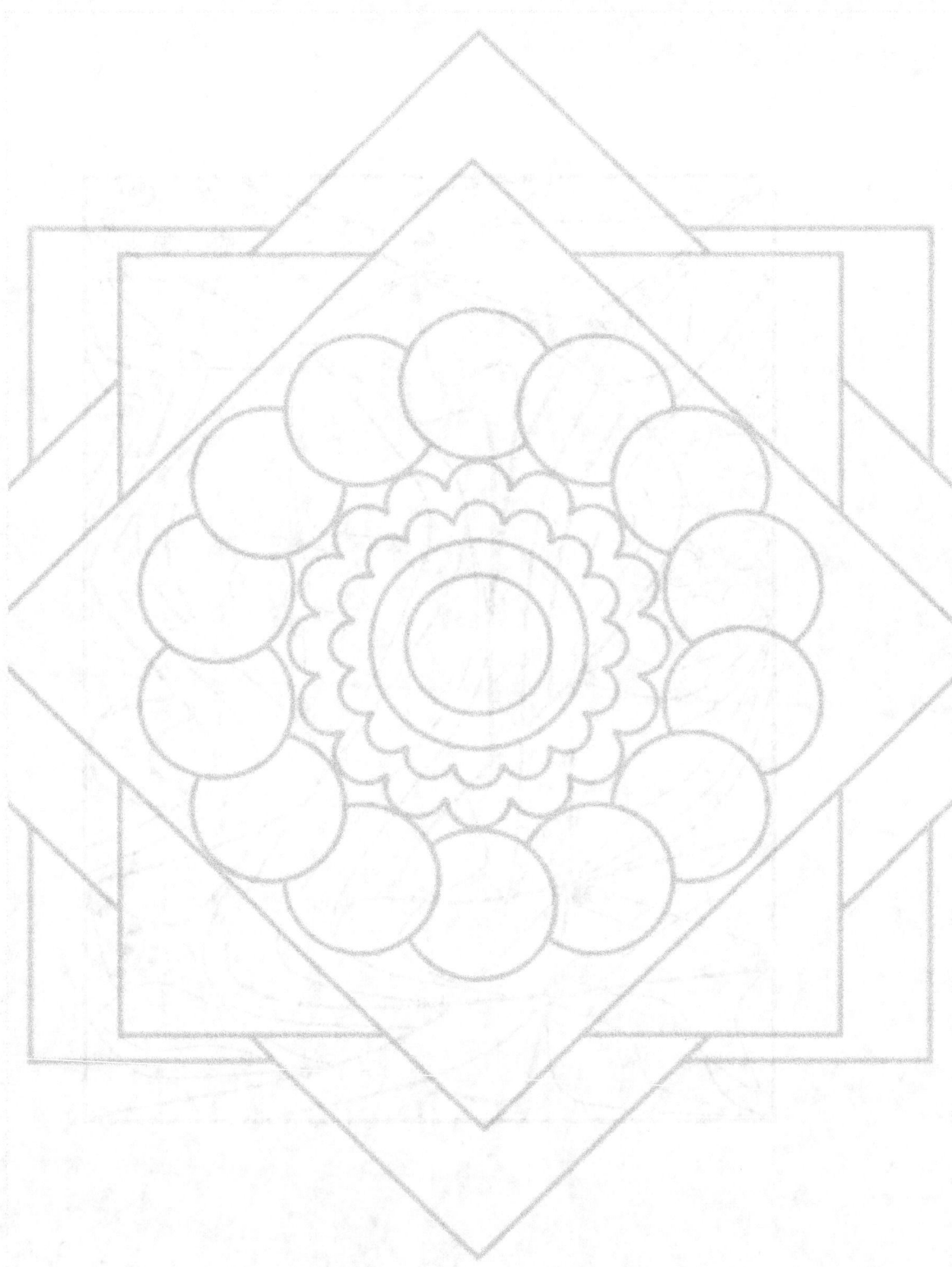

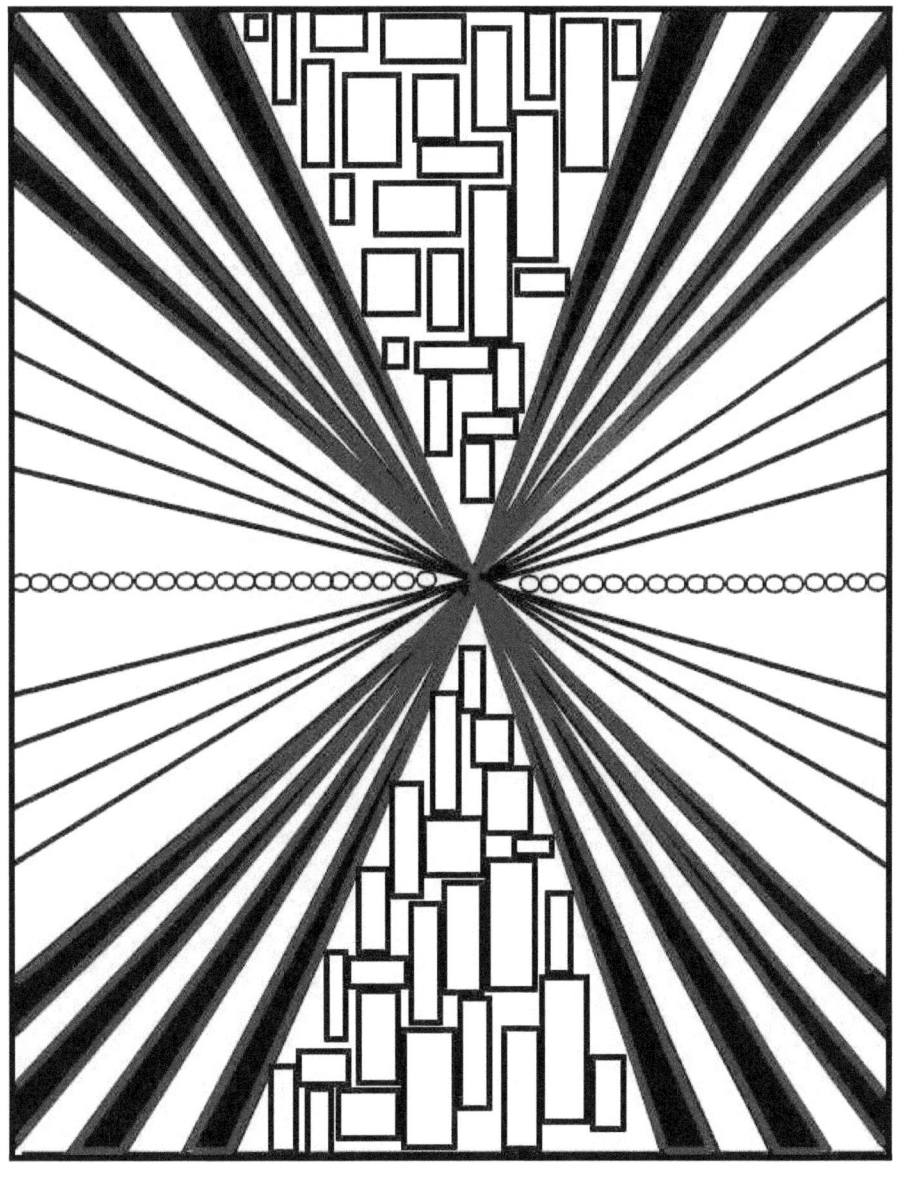

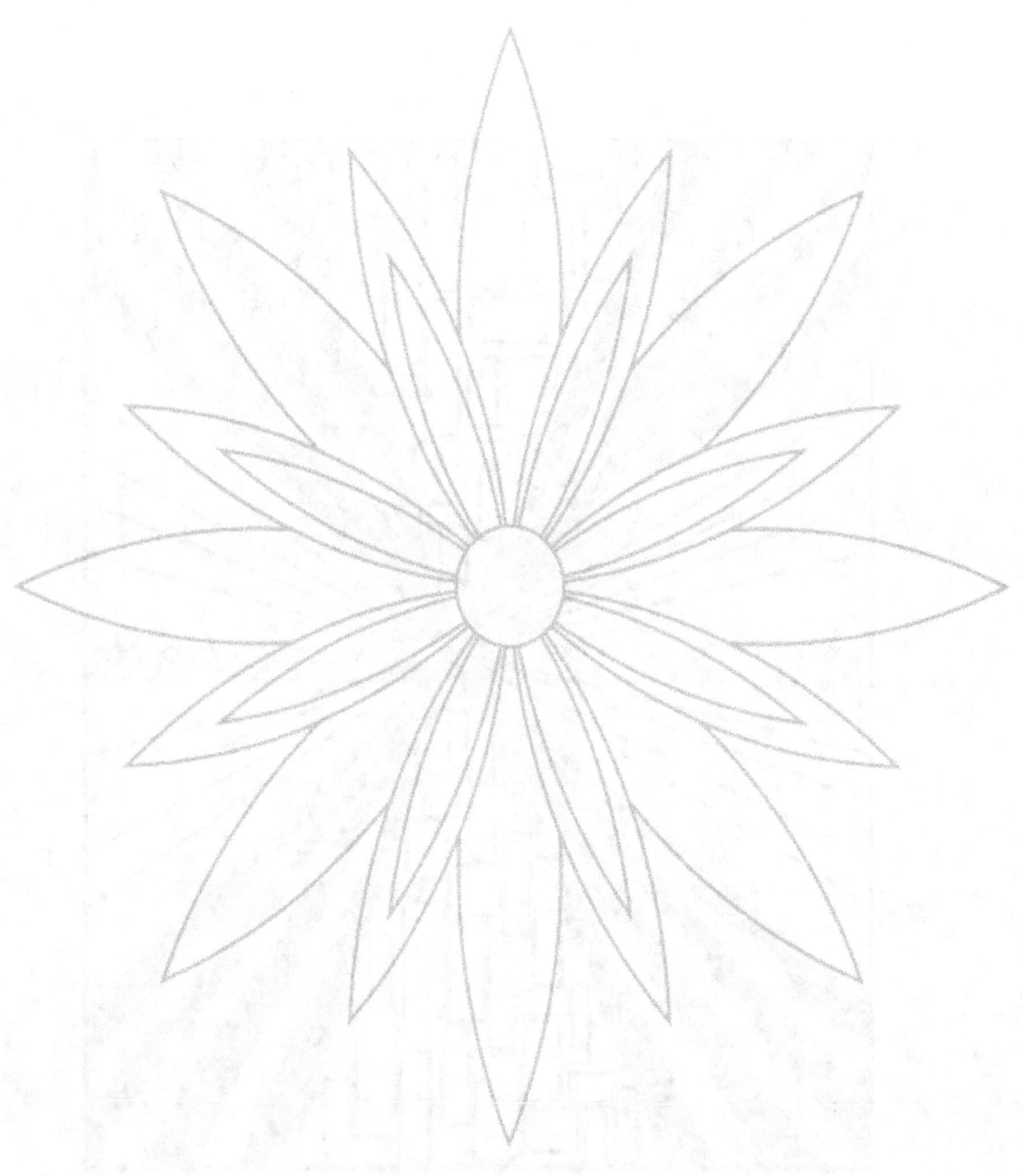

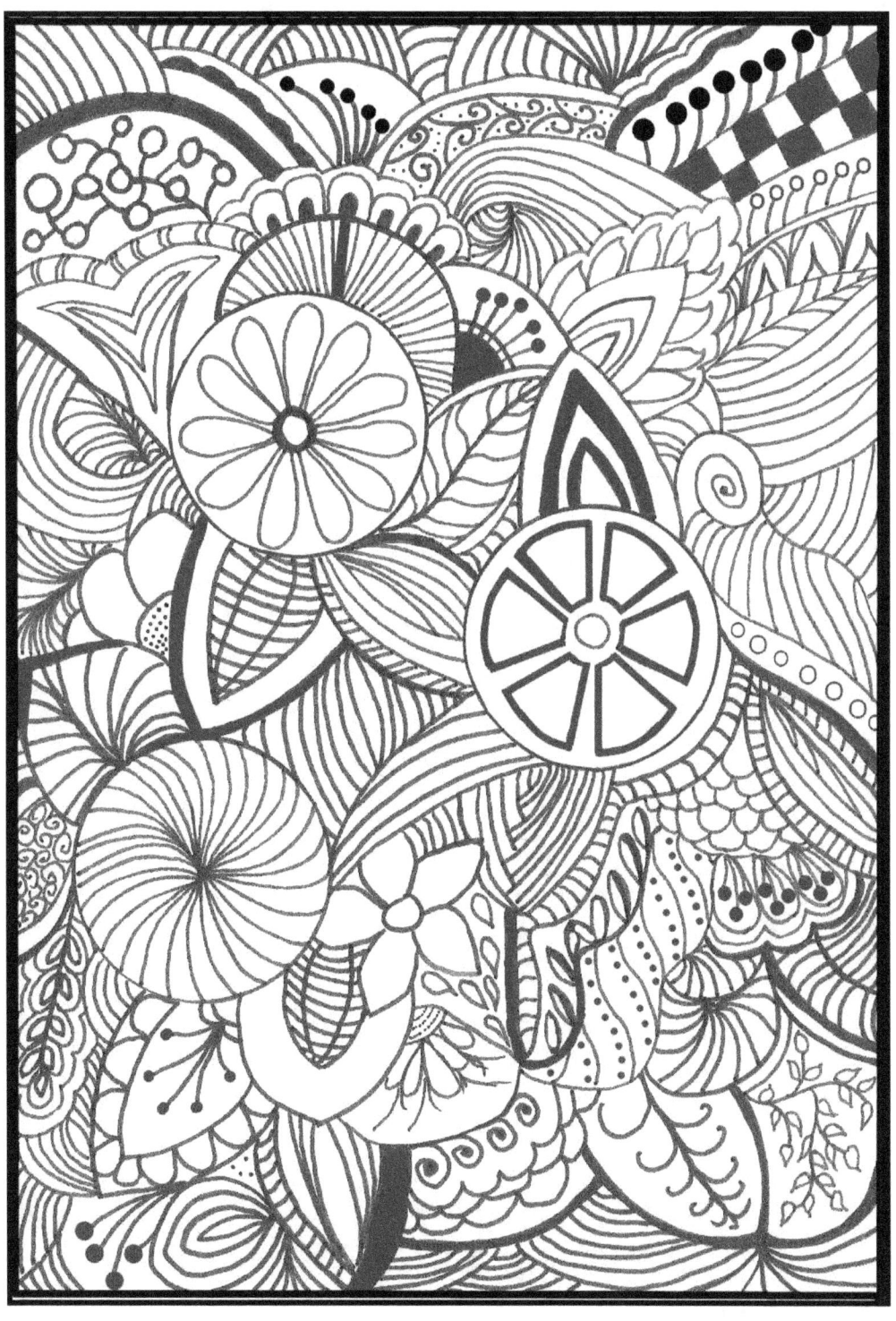

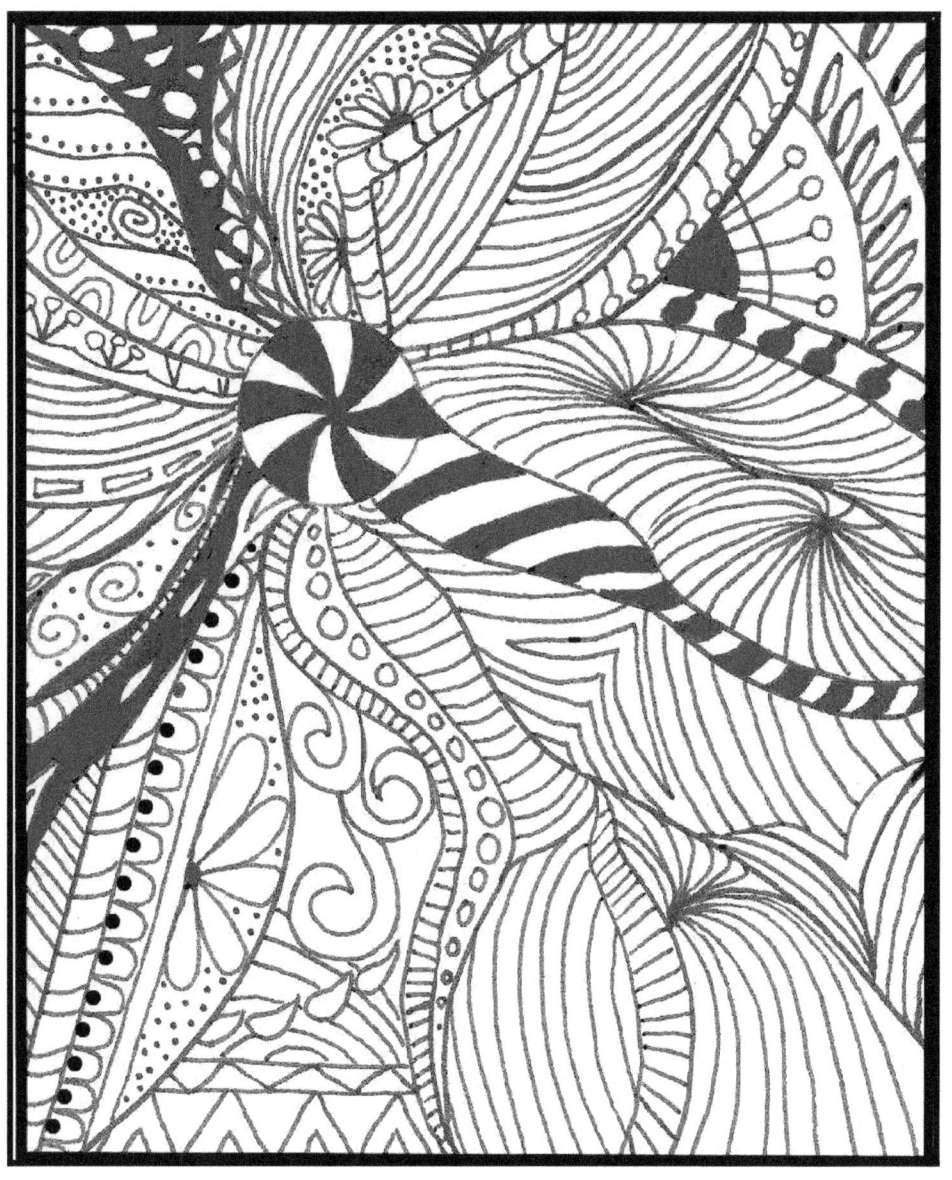

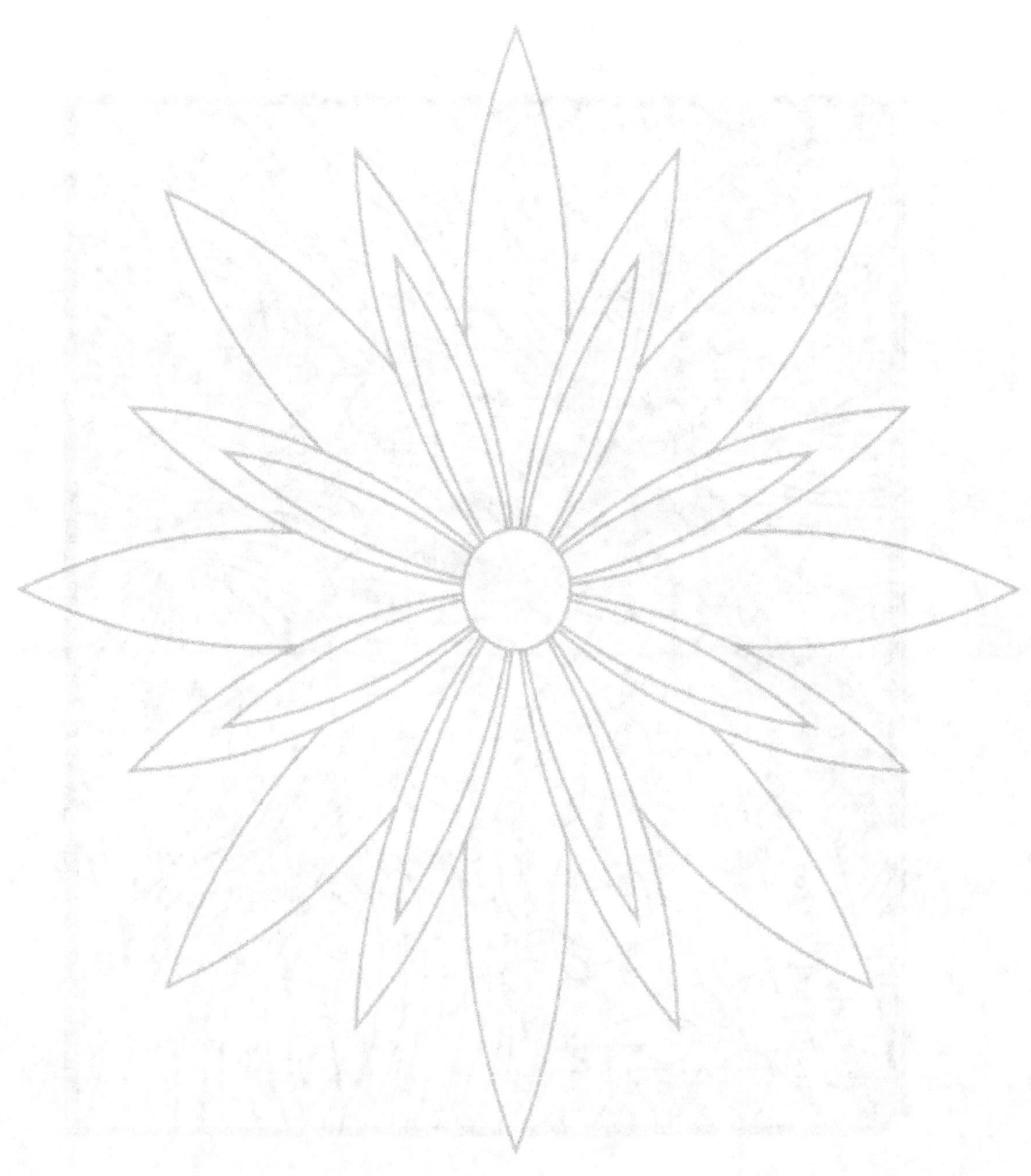

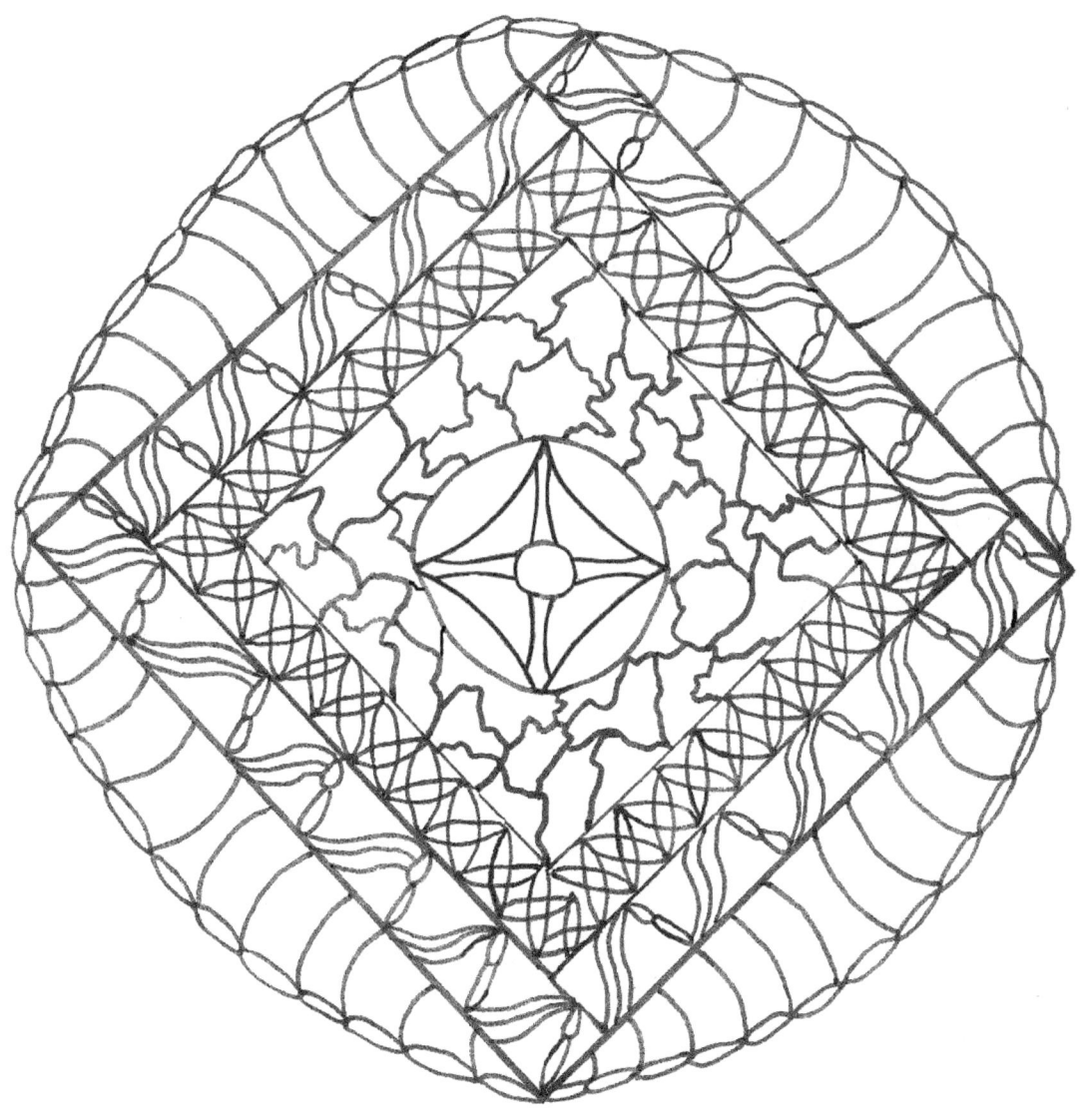

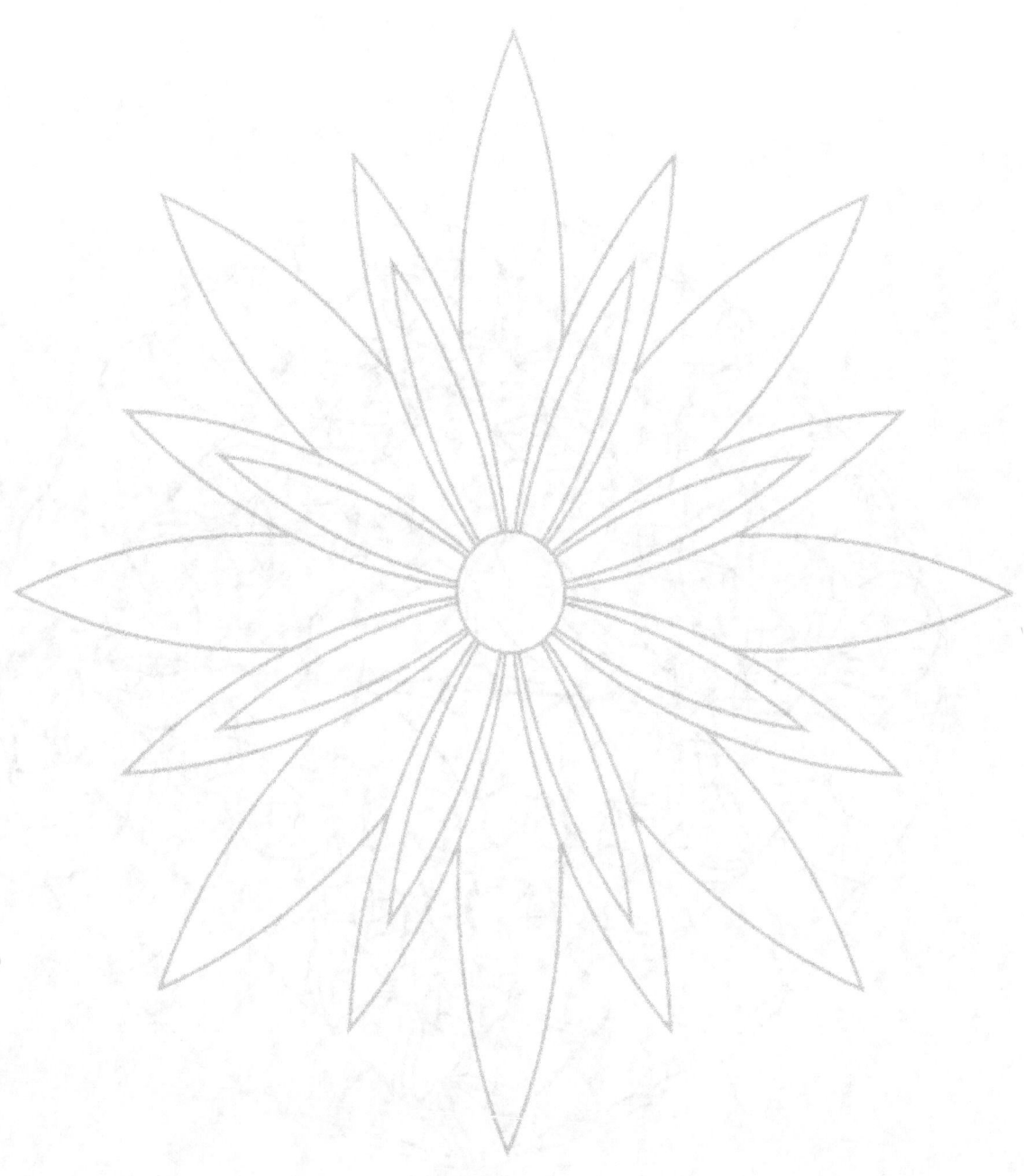

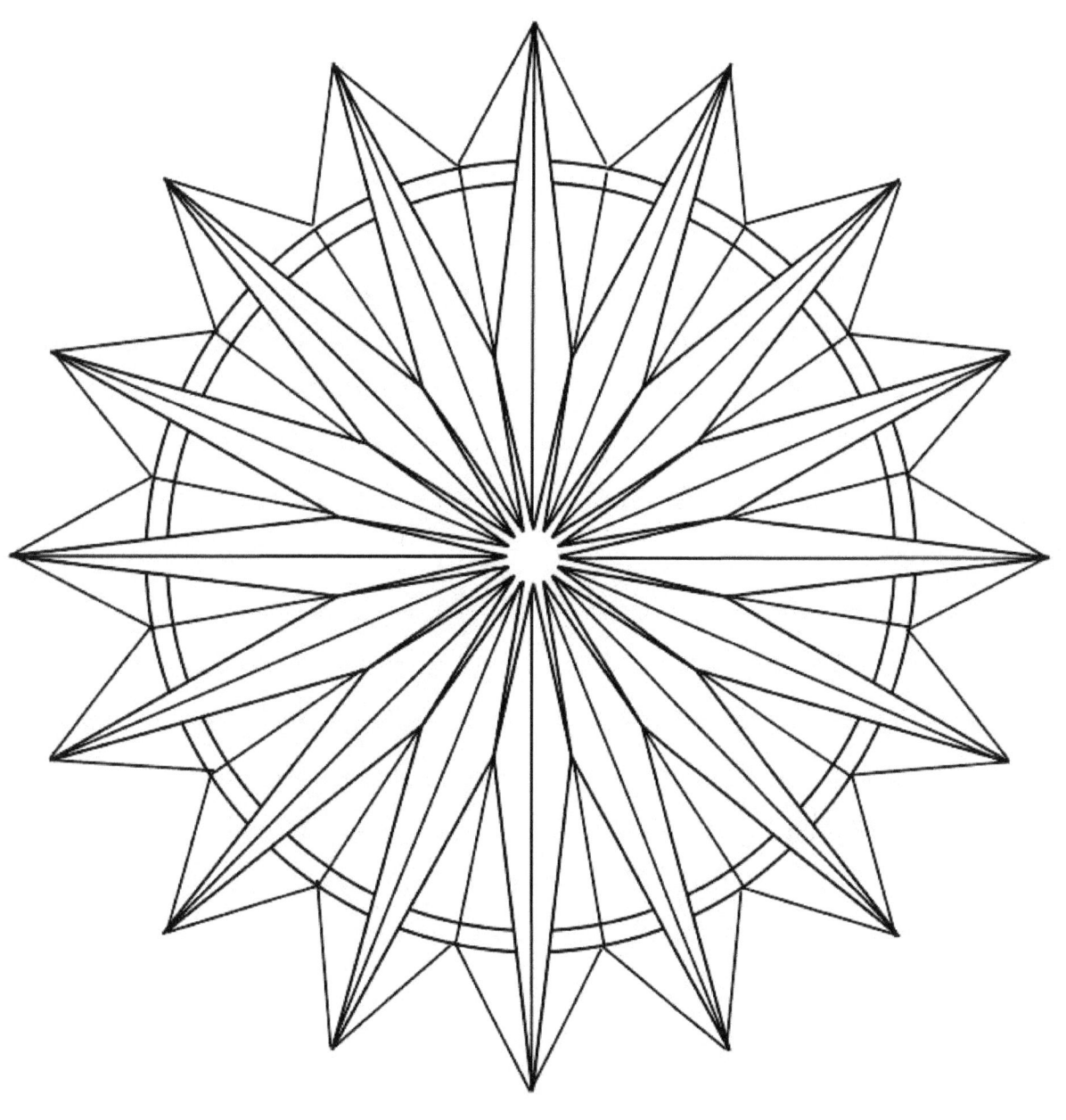

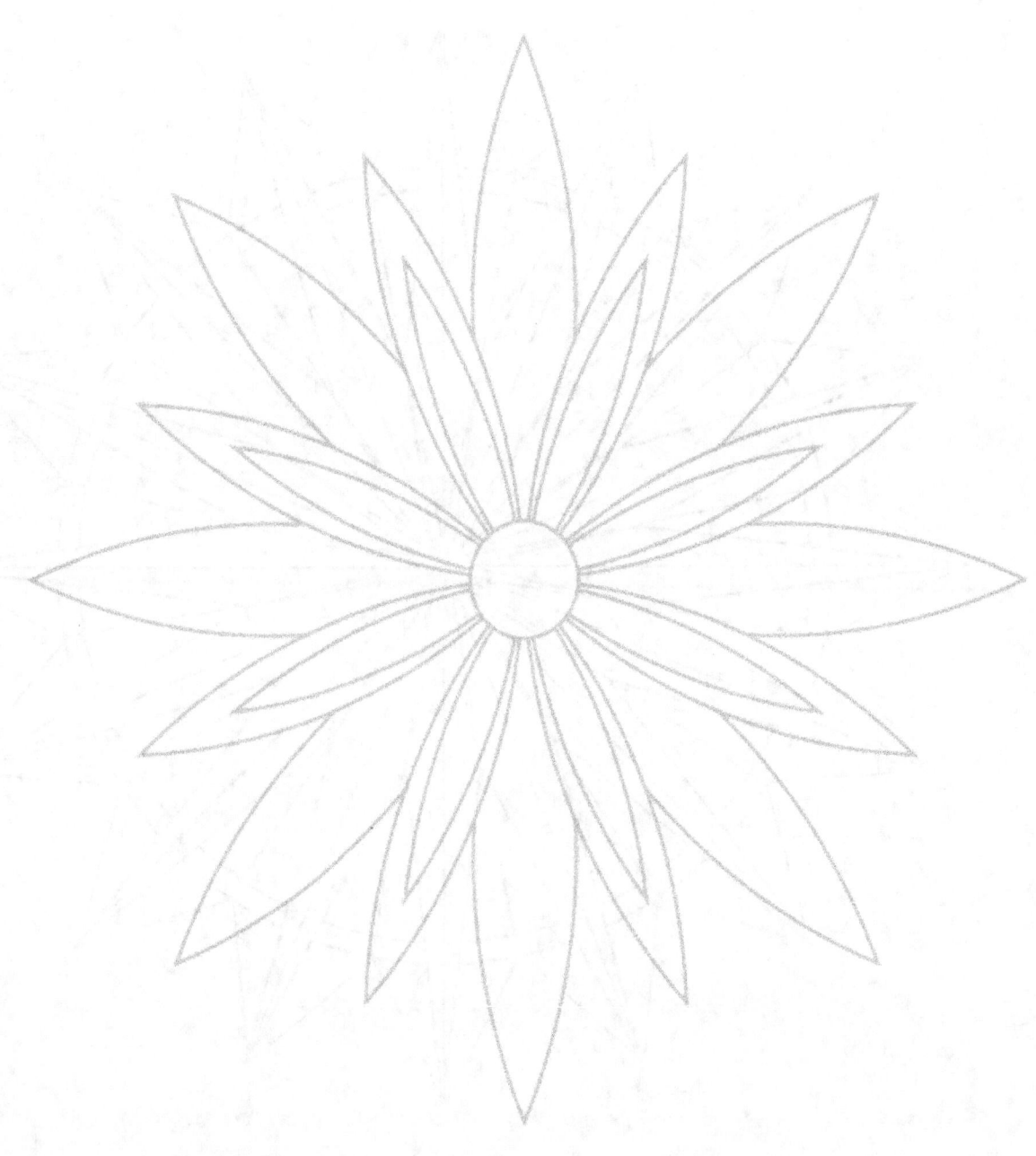

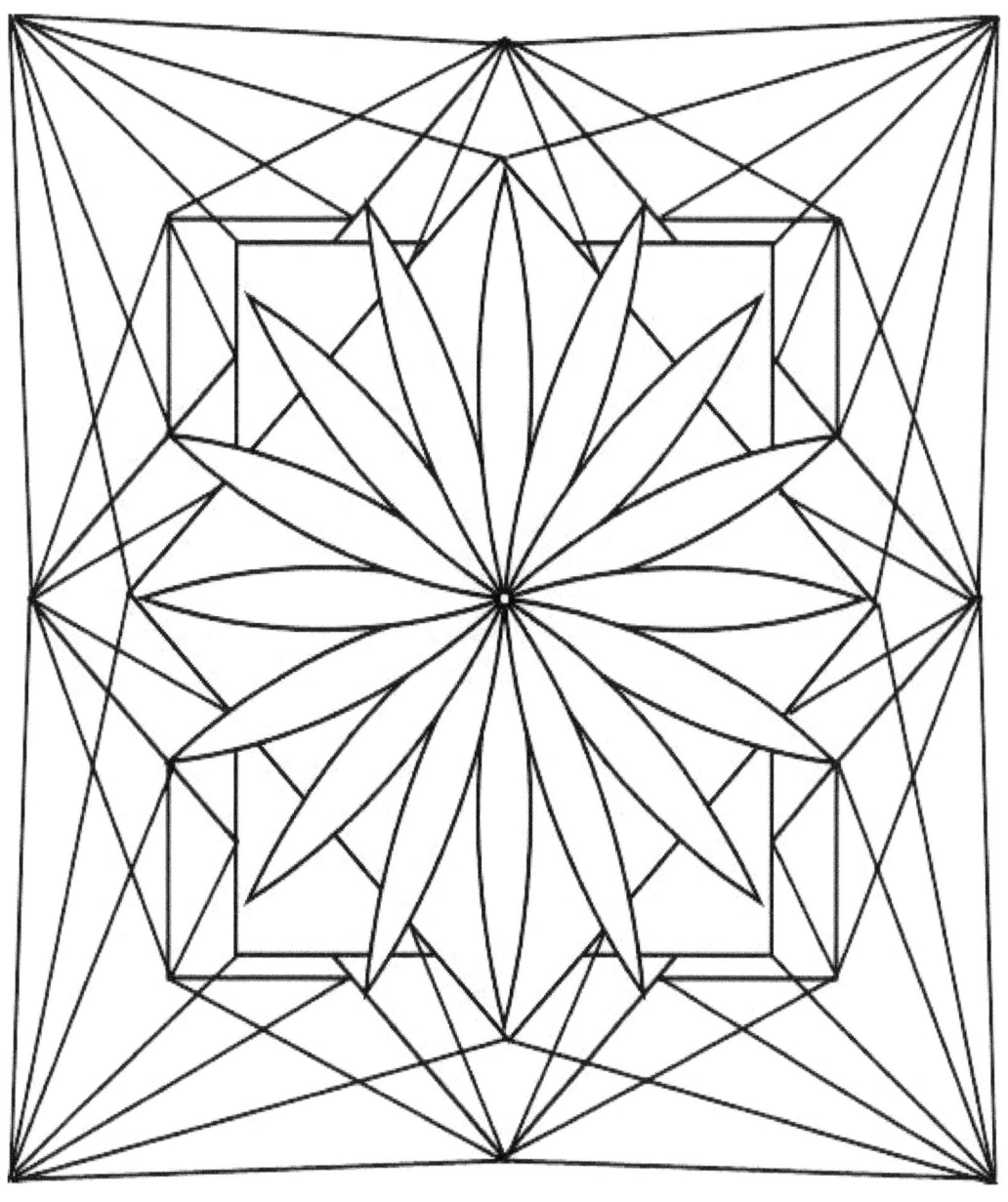

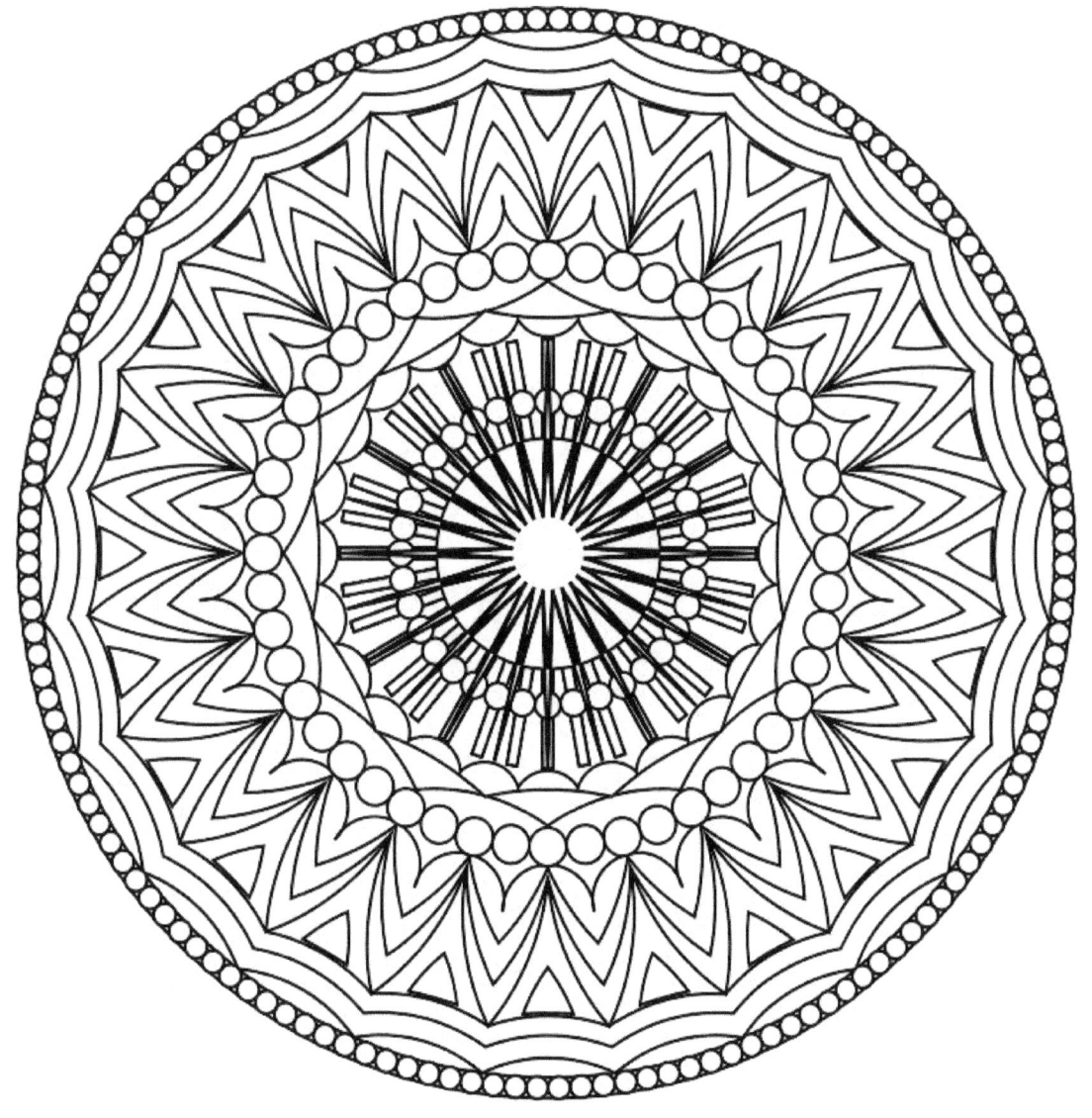

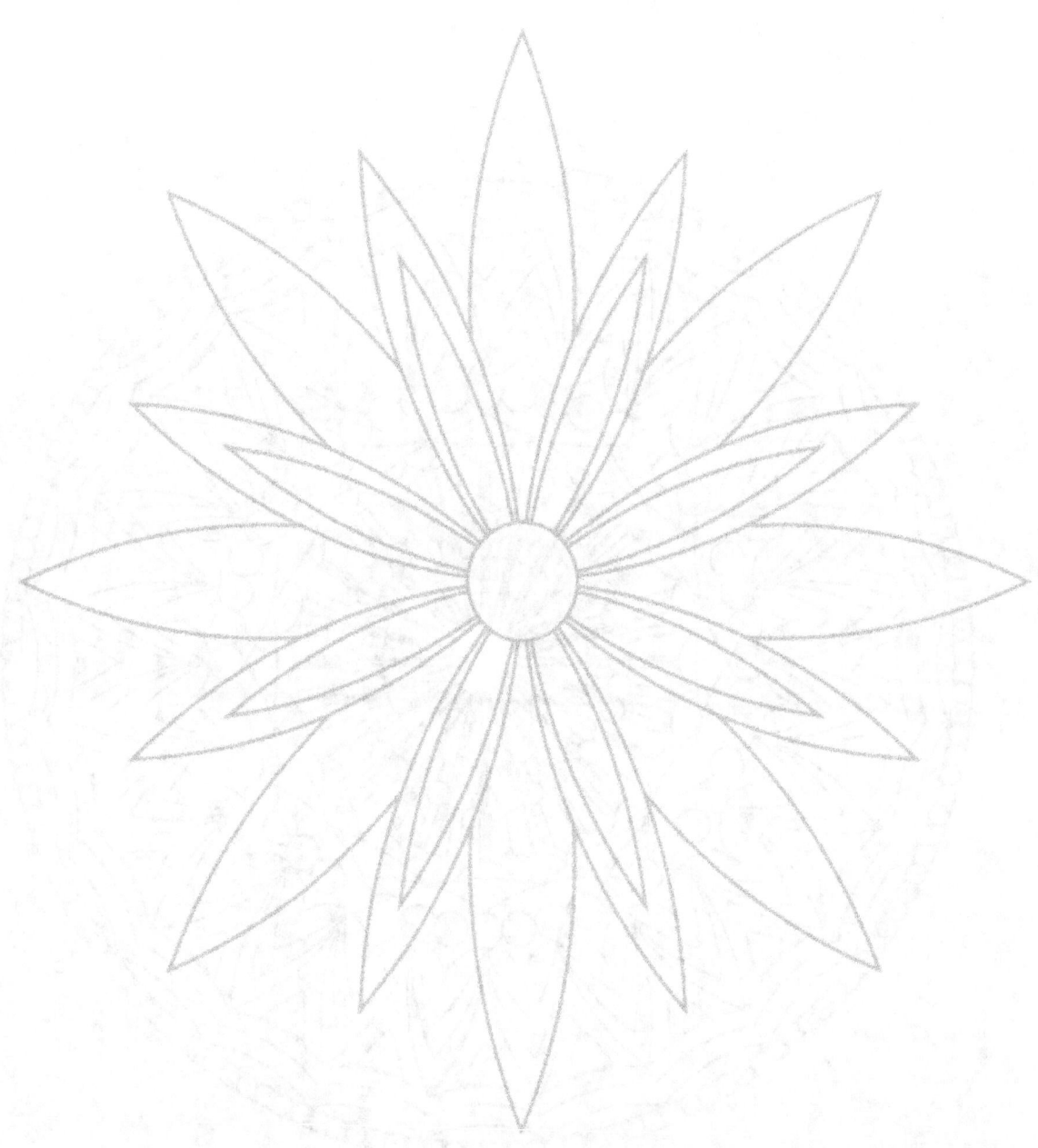

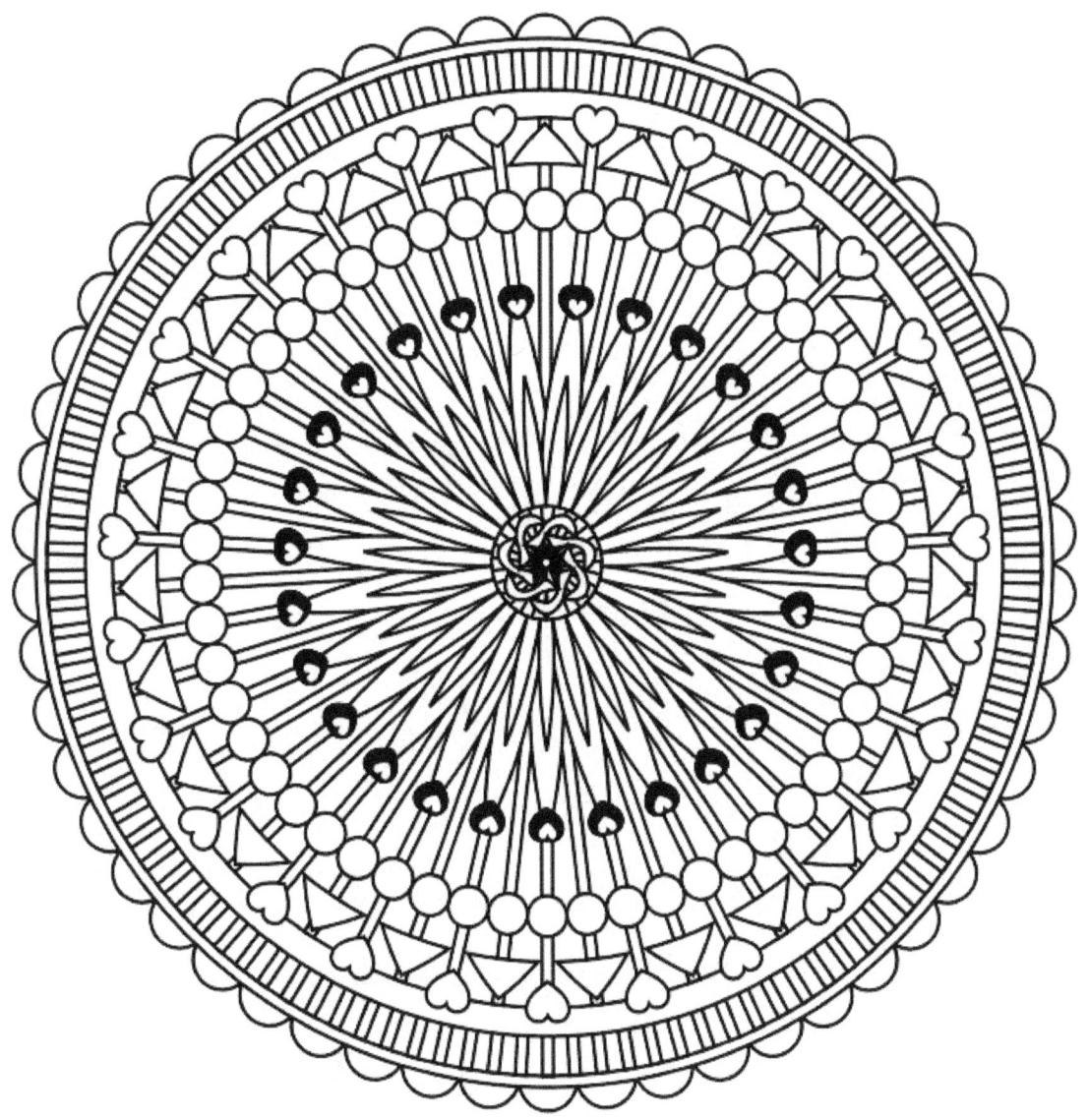

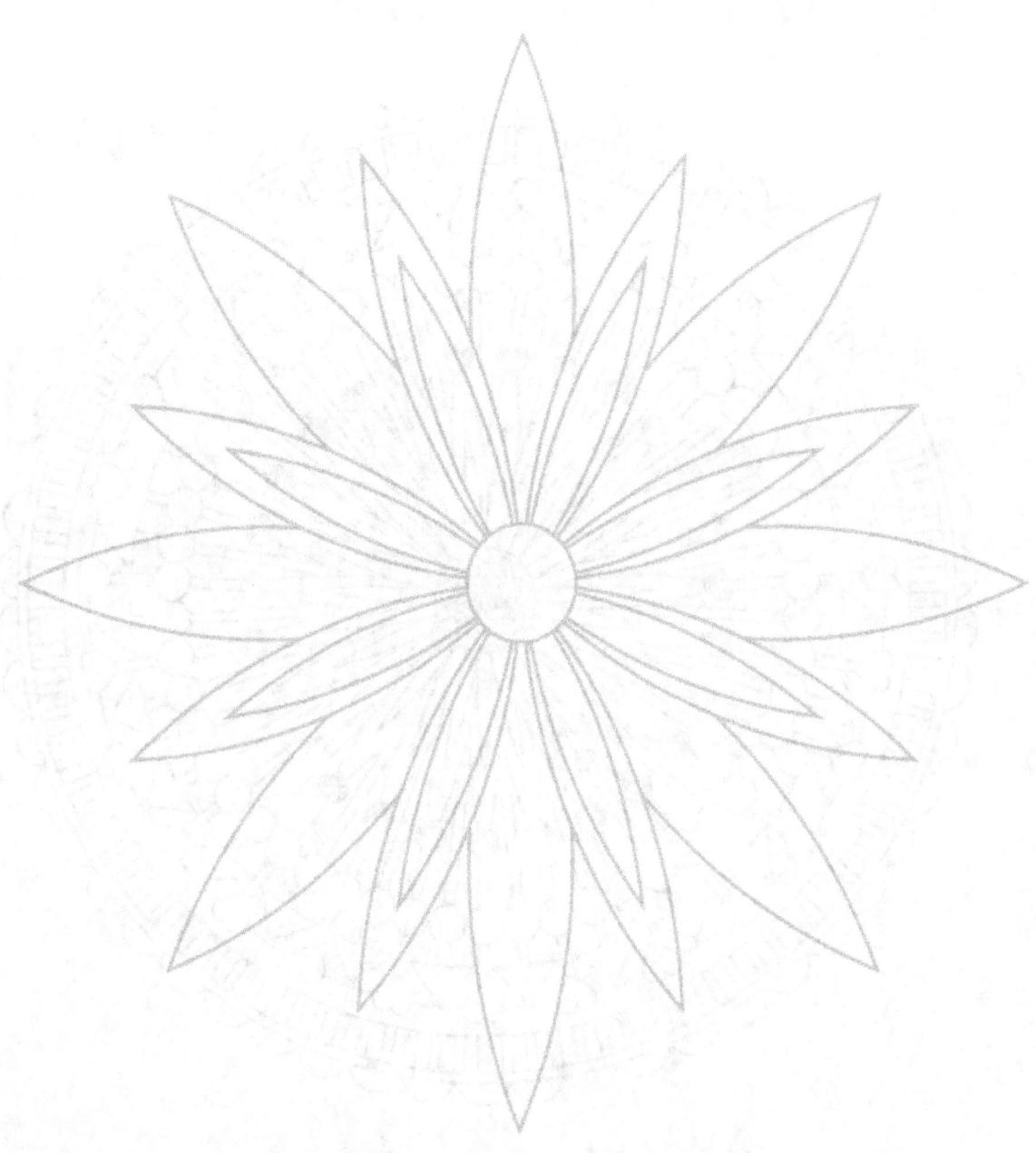

More paperback coloring books can be sourced through

KD COLORING STUDIO AT

http://kdcoloring.com

www.ingramcontent.com/pod-product-compliance
Lightning Source LLC
Chambersburg PA
CBHW080606180526
45168CB00007B/2801